STECK-VAUGHN
CRITICAL THI

Reading, Thinking, and Reasoning Skills

Authors

Don Barnes
Professor of Education
Ball State University; Muncie, Indiana

Arlene Burgdorf
Former Resource Consultant
Hammond Indiana Public Schools

L. Stanley Wenck
Professor of Educational Psychology
Ball State University; Muncie, Indiana

Consultant

Gloria Sesso
Supervisor of Social Studies
Half Hollow Hills School District; Dix Hills, New York

			LEVEL		
A	B	C	D	E	F

STECK-VAUGHN
ELEMENTARY · SECONDARY · ADULT · LIBRARY
A Harcourt Company

www.steck-vaughn.com

ACKNOWLEDGMENTS

Executive Editor
Elizabeth Strauss

Project Editor
Anita Arndt

Consulting Editor
Melinda Veatch

Design, Production, and Editorial Services
The Quarasan Group, Inc.

Contributing Writers
Tara McCarthy
Linda Ward Beech

Cover Design
Linda Adkins Graphic Design

Text:
Every effort has been made to trace the ownership of all copyrighted material and to secure the necessary permissions to reprint these selections. In the event of any question arising as to the use of any material, the editor and publisher, while expressing regret for any inadvertent error, will be happy to make the necessary correction in future printings.

Excerpt from THE PEOPLE, YES, copyright 1936 by Harcourt Brace Jovanovich, Inc.; renewed 1964 by Carl Sandburg. Reprinted by permission of the publisher.

Photography:
p. 5 — H. Armstrong Roberts
p. 14 — NASA
p. 27 — Nita Winter
p. 49 — Nita Winter
p. 67 — H. Armstrong Roberts
p. 87 — Nita Winter
p. 109 — H. Armstrong Roberts

Illustration:
pp. 6, 31, 94, 98 — Ruth Brunke
pp. 7, 29, 41, 53, 122 — Linda Hawkins
pp. 8, 17, 21, 37, 65, 79, 79, 84, 120, 126 — Barbara Lanza/Carol Bancroft & Friends
pp. 18, 19, 33, 39, 45, 52, 54, 57, 66, 70, 75, 77, 81, 85, 86, 91, 93, 97, 100, 110, 111, 113, 115, 117, 122, 124 — Lonestar Studio
pp. 24, 35, 60, 83, 107 — Scott Bieser
pp. 26, 28, 76, 121 — Liz Allen
pp. 42, 48, 55, 62, 73, 88, 103, 108, 114, 116, 123 — Jackie Rogers/Carol Bancroft & Friends
p. 51 — Nancy Walter

ISBN 0–8114–6603–5

TABLE OF CONTENTS

TABLE OF CONTENTS

Knowing

Knowing means getting the facts together. Let's try it out. Look at the picture. What is the boy holding? Do you think he made the object? How can you tell? Look at the expression on the boy's face. What does it tell you?

To **classify** means to group things that are alike in some way.

In some sports, an official game can only be played with five or more people. In other sports, you need only one or two people.

tennis	basketball	football
soccer	fishing	golf	baseball

A. Write the name of each sport listed in the box under the proper heading.

Five or More People   **One or Two People**

1. _____   2. _____

_____   _____

_____   _____

B. Write the names of three sports that can be classified under the headings listed below.

Played on a Court   **Played on a Field**

_____   _____

_____   _____

_____   _____

Name _____

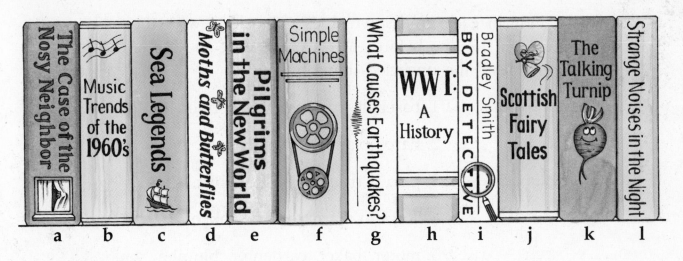

a   b   c   d   e   f   g   h   i   j   k   l

A. Bill's mother likes to read books about science, his brother likes to read mysteries, and his sister likes to read folklore. Write the letter of the books read by each member of Bill's family.

    1. **Mother**   2. **Brother**   3. **Sister**

       _____   _____   _____

       _____   _____   _____

       _____   _____   _____

B. Read the book titles that have not been classified above. These books belong to Bill.

    1. List the letters of the remaining books: _____ _____ _____

    2. What type of book does Bill like to read? _____

C. What type of book do you like to read?

_____

_____

Name _____

A. Circle the item in each group that does not belong with the other items. Then, on the line before each group, write the name of the group to which all the uncircled items belong.

_____ 1. baseball, rocking horse, ruler, top, marbles

_____ 2. harp, piano, clarinet, flute, pillow

_____ 3. jacket, trousers, nose, shirt, shoes

_____ 4. Toronto, Paris, Brazil, Tokyo

_____ 5. motor, baker, carpenter, plumber, tailor

B. Above the blanks are four words that could describe the objects listed. These words name some of the objects' possible characteristics. On the lines after each word, check the characteristics that might fit. (Some objects will have more characteristics listed than others.)

	Round	Colorful	Plaything	Sewed
1. baseball	a. _____	b. _____	c. _____	d. _____
2. globe	a. _____	b. _____	c. _____	d. _____
3. marble	a. _____	b. _____	c. _____	d. _____

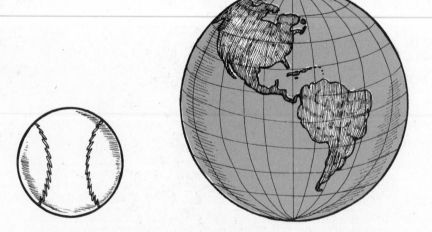

Name _____

A. Most of the words in the groups below have something in common.
   Some words are out of place. **First**, cross out two words in each list
   that do **not** belong. **Next**, write a word to name each group in the box
   above each list. **Last**, write each word that was crossed out below the
   group to which it belongs.

poodle	wren	tuna
perch	cardinal	beagle
collie	bloodhound	trout
dove	canary	blue jay
Irish setter	herring	salmon
cocker spaniel	pigeon	bass

B. The words at the bottom of the page belong in three groups. Write the
   words on the lines below to make three groups. Then, give each group
   a name which fits all the items. The first name has been chosen for you.

Rivers		

Nile, oak, pine, Hudson, Asia, birch, Amazon,
North America, maple, Africa, Europe, Mississippi

Name

9

A. Nine ways to group items are listed in the box. Write the group letter on the line before each item below. Find at least two group letters for each item. The first one is done for you.

> a. made of wood   b. made of metal   c. a tool   d. a food
> e. soft   f. made of cloth   g. made of clay   h. round
>   i. long and narrow

___d, e, i___ 1. banana   _____ 9. needle

_____ 2. spoon   _____ 10. orange

_____ 3. yardstick   _____ 11. pitcher

_____ 4. toothpick   _____ 12. blanket

_____ 5. ring   _____ 13. tablecloth

_____ 6. towel   _____ 14. scissors

_____ 7. saw   _____ 15. spaghetti

_____ 8. broom   _____ 16. scarf

B. Decide how these items can be classified into three groups. Then, on the lines below, write the group names.

> viper, lilies, Mexico, Japan, zinnia, cobra, Canada,
> python, petunia, marigold, Cuba, boa constrictor

_____   _____   _____

Name _____

Critical Thinking, Level D © 1993 Steck-Vaughn

A. Write **R** before each sentence that tells something that could be real. Write **F** before each sentence that has a fanciful meaning.

1. _____ Santiago made up a story about a monster.

   _____ Santiago met a monster in the woods.

2. _____ The purple cow gave more milk than the white cow.

   _____ We read a poem about a purple cow.

3. _____ The dragon belched fire from its jaws.

   _____ Dragons are creatures in storybooks.

B. In each story below, underline the statement or statements that could be real.

1. Amparo was getting ready to fix the door that squeaked. She reached for a screwdriver, but the door reached out and grabbed it from her. "Wait," it said. "You don't need that. All I need is a little oil."

2. Jake was taking a walk in the forest. He saw a two-foot-tall man dressed in green standing beneath a tree. Jake picked up the little man and said, "Now, Mr. Leprechaun, you must lead me to your treasure!"

3. Chen gave his cat a bowl of milk. "No, thank you," said the cat. "I prefer water." Then the cat jumped up on the sink and lapped up some water from the dripping faucet.

4. A sea sprite sat on the rocks and watched Myra swim. Myra was scared and began to swim away. "Don't go," begged the sea sprite. "I only want to be friends."

Name

A. The quotes below are from a book called The People, Yes by Carl Sandburg. Each of the quotes is fanciful because it exaggerates the truth so much. On the line below each quote, rewrite the quote so that it is closer to reality.

"They have yarns" . . .

1. "Of a skyscraper so tall they had to put hinges on the two top stories so to let the moon go by,"

_____

2. "Of pancakes so thin they had only one side,"

_____

3. "Of the herd of cattle in California getting lost in a giant tree that had hollowed out,"

_____

B. Place a check before the statements below that are fanciful.

_____ 1. Because the beans grew so high, Dora had to climb them in order to touch their tops.

_____ 2. Early in the morning, bison, elk, and deer came to drink from the pond.

_____ 3. Many varieties of colored fish swam in the water.

_____ 4. For his birthday, Jim got a poodle that could count.

_____ 5. That evening after the performance, the circus animals discussed the audience.

Name

_____

Statements that can be proved true are called **facts**. Statements that describe only what someone thinks or believes are called **opinions**.

A. On the line before each fact sentence below, write **F**. On the line before each opinion sentence, write **O**.

_____ 1. It's better to have a picnic in the park than here.

_____ 2. There are thirty-six inches in a yard.

_____ 3. We must never plan a field trip on Friday.

_____ 4. More of the earth's surface is water than land.

_____ 5. Some clocks are run by batteries.

_____ 6. Our art class does better work than any other class.

_____ 7. In the 1400s, many people thought that the earth was flat.

_____ 8. A dozen is the same as twelve.

_____ 9. All books must be worth reading.

_____ 10. Everyone should take up aerobic dancing.

B. Certain words signal that an opinion is coming. Some examples are **should, better, must**. Find and circle these words in the sentences you marked **O** in exercise A. Then use these words to rewrite the following sentences and make them opinions.

1. Students can learn how to play an instrument.

_____

2. They can then play in the school band.

_____

Name _____

A. Write **F** on the line before each sentence that is a fact (a fact can be proved to be true). Put **O** on the line if the sentence gives someone's opinion. For each **O** sentence, circle the word or words which make you think that the sentence is an opinion.

———— 1. Neil Armstrong was the first person on the moon.

———— 2. Gloria's report on toads was very well done.

———— 3. Being a pilot must be a dangerous job.

———— 4. You should use red paint on your porch.

———— 5. Thomas Edison invented the electric light.

———— 6. Everyone likes pecan pie for dessert.

B. Rewrite the sentences from A. Write the fact sentences so that they express an opinion. Write the opinion sentences so that they tell a fact.

1. _____

2. _____

3. _____

4. _____

5. _____

6. _____

Name _____

Read the story below. On the lines below the story, write four facts and four opinions from the story.

A man, his son, and a donkey were traveling to market.

A farmer saw them and said, "You should be riding that animal." The boy got onto the donkey.

Soon, they met a group of men. "Lazy boy," one called, "you should let your father ride." The son got down and his father got on the donkey.

By and by, they met a woman who exclaimed, "You are mean. You should not make that boy walk." So the man took the boy up behind him.

Shortly, the travelers came to a village. Immediately, people began shouting, "Ungrateful wretches! That poor animal should not have to carry both of you." They both got off.

The man and the boy had a difficult time trying to decide what to do. Finally, they tied the donkey's feet together, put a pole between the donkey's legs, and carried the donkey.

Soon, someone along the road yelled, "I think that anyone would have to be stupid to carry a donkey."

The man and his son gave up in disgust.

Facts

1. _____

2. _____

3. _____

4. _____

Opinions

1. _____

2. _____

3. _____

4. _____

Name _____

Read the news article. Then write a letter to the editor of the paper stating your opinion.

Will Wishton Become Wishing Wells?
Many Wish It Would; Others Wish It Wasn't So

If wishes come true, then the town of Wishton may soon change its name to Wishing Wells. A vote was taken by the city council last night to approve the name change. It is hoped that the new name would draw attention—and thus tourists—to the town's famous wishing well.

"People will come here from all over to see the well, toss in their coins, and make a wish," said council member Jim Hayes. "A new name will clear up any confusion about where that well is."

It is a well-known fact that many people now confuse Wishton with Wishington and never get here to see the wishing well. However, not everyone agrees with Mr. Hayes about changing the town name. "There's a lot more to this town than a wishing well," said Anna Riglio. "We've been known as Wishton for 150 years. I don't think we should change."

A demonstration for Wishton fans is planned for tomorrow afternoon at the wishing well.

Dear Editor:

_____

_____

_____

_____

_____

_____

Name _____

Critical Thinking, Level D © 1993 Steck-Vaughn

A **definition** gives the meaning of a word. An **example** is the name of an item belonging to the group. Several definitions and examples are listed below for the words **cat**, **fish**, and **bird**. Put **D** before the best definition at the left. Put **E** before the example at the right which fits.

I. cat:

_____ A. a member of the cat family   _____ 1. Persian

_____ B. an animal with four legs, claws,   _____ 2. Scottie
a long tail, and fur
          _____ 3. sparrow
_____ C. a kitty which is kept for a pet

II. fish:

_____ A. an animal that lives in water   _____ 1. turtle

_____ B. a vertebrate that lives in water   _____ 2. frog
and has gills
          _____ 3. trout
_____ C. an animal covered with scales

III. bird:

_____ A. an animal that flies   _____ 1. bee

_____ B. an animal that lays eggs   _____ 2. sparrow

_____ C. a warm-blooded animal with feathers   _____ 3. butterfly
and wings that lays eggs

Name

A **definition** gives the meaning of a word. Read the definitions in group **A**. Look in group **B** to find the word that matches the definition. Write the letter of the word on the line before the definition. In group **C**, give two examples for each definition. The first one is done for you.

A

_c_ 1. material used in the body to sustain growth and provide energy

_____ 2. inner parts of the body that perform a special function

_____ 3. a woody plant with a long stem and deep roots

_____ 4. implements used in a kitchen to prepare food

_____ 5. devices used to produce sound

_____ 6. any way of exchanging information from one person to another

B

a. tree

b. musical instruments

c. food

d. communication

e. vital organs

f. cooking utensils

C

1. ___vegetables___
   ___fruits___

2. _____

   _____

3. _____

   _____

4. _____

   _____

5. _____

   _____

6. _____

   _____

Name _____

Critical Thinking, Level D © 1993 Steck-Vaughn

To **define** a word is to give its meaning. A **fruit** is an edible (good to eat) product of a tree, bush, shrub, or vine. **Examples** of a word are illustrations of the kinds of items that belong to the group being defined. Apples, pears, bananas, and peaches are examples of fruits.

A. On the line before each sentence, write **D** if the sentence gives definitions. Write **E** if the sentence gives examples.

_____ 1. A mammal is an animal that gives milk to its young.

_____ 2. A rooster or hen is a fowl.

_____ 3. A bird which imitates the calls of other birds is the mockingbird.

_____ 4. Furniture refers to items such as beds, tables, or desks.

_____ 5. An emu is a large, three-toed Australian bird.

B. For each word, write a definition on line 1, and write at least two examples on line 2. You may use a dictionary.

a. **entertainer**   1. _____

                       2. _____

b. **book**   1. _____

                       2. _____

c. **airplane**   1. _____

                       2. _____

d. **teacher**   1. _____

                       2. _____

Name _____

Read the definition in each paragraph. Then write an example of your own on the lines.

1. Friendship is the admiration and affection that two friends have for one another. In friendship, two people have an understanding and are willing to help each other out as well as share good times together.

   An example is

   _____

   _____

   _____

2. Courage is a quality that means someone has the strength to meet danger or hardship. Someone who has courage is firm of purpose and can overcome fear.

   An example is

   _____

   _____

   _____

3. A sense of humor has to do with someone's sense of fun. A sense of humor also has to do with someone's ability to see the wit and laughter in things.

   An example is

   _____

   _____

   _____

Name _____

Critical Thinking, Level D © 1993 Steck-Vaughn

A. Read each paragraph below. Then write two facts from the paragraph that support the main idea. Last of all, write each person's name under his or her mask.

Our class had fun with the paper-bag masks we made. One lunch hour we put on our masks and marched around the cafeteria. The other students loved it. Then we displayed our masks in the hallway.

Main Idea: Our class had fun with paper-bag masks.

1. _____

2. _____

Our masks showed great variety. Debbie's mask had a wide mouth and no hair. Jeff's mask had slanting eyes. Holly's mask looked like a girl wearing a headband, and Greg's mask looked sad.

Main Idea: The masks showed great variety.

1. _____

2. _____

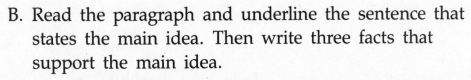

B. Read the paragraph and underline the sentence that states the main idea. Then write three facts that support the main idea.

The ostrich is the largest living bird. An ostrich may be as much as eight feet (2.4m) tall and weigh three hundred pounds (135kg). Females lay eggs that weigh as much as three pounds (1.35kg).

1. _____

2. _____

3. _____

Name _____

An **outline** is the frame or skeleton of a paragraph or an article. It shows how something is organized.

Fill in the outlines below. Follow the directions given for each part. Main topics have Roman numerals before them. Capital letters are used for subtopics.

A. Below are four main topics.

Ways of transporting coal
Formation of coal
Types of mines
Preparing coal

Write each main topic in a blank so that it fits the facts (subtopics) below it. The first one is done for you.

I. ___Formation of coal___
   A. Plant life died
   B. It rotted
   C. Pressure was applied

II. _____
   A. Surface
   B. Underground

III. _____
   A. Remove rocks
   B. Make pieces smaller
   C. Wash

IV. _____
   A. Railroads
   B. River barges

B. Below are some facts (subtopics) about rabbits. Write the facts (subtopics) on the lines under the main heading each one fits.

Feed at night, Jackrabbit, Long ears, Kick and bite, Chisellike teeth, Cottontail, Strong hind legs

I. Appearance of rabbits
   A. _____
   B. _____
   C. _____

II. Habits of rabbits
   A. _____
   B. _____

III. Kinds of rabbits
   A. _____
   B. _____

Name

Critical Thinking, Level D © 1993 Steck-Vaughn

Read the article below.

Planting a Garden

First, choose a spot of ground where plants will grow well. The ground should be fairly fertile. It should get plenty of sunshine. Pick a spot where you can bring water to the plants.

After you have chosen a garden spot, get the soil ready for planting. Scatter fertilizer over the ground. Next, dig up the ground and break up any large clumps of soil. Then, rake the soil until it is fine and the garden plot is level.

Now you are ready to plant some seeds. Dig the holes in straight rows. Place seeds an equal distance apart as the seed package shows. Cover the seeds with soil. Water the garden if rain does not come. Soon you should have some plants.

Follow these directions for making an outline.

1. Look at the first sentence of each paragraph to find the main idea. Write a main idea after each Roman numeral.

2. Write other facts on the lines below the main idea.

3. Begin each line with a capital letter.

I. _____

   A. _____

   B. _____

   C. _____

II. _____

   A. _____

   B. _____

   C. _____

   D. _____

III. _____

   A. _____

   B. _____

   C. _____

   D. _____

Name _____

A **summary** is a restatement of the main points of a paragraph or an article.

Read the paragraph. Then complete the summary below it using key words from the paragraph.

The first handkerchiefs were used in ancient Rome. Only rich people could afford these white linen cloths, and they used them mainly for wiping their brows. When it became cheaper to make these cloths, ordinary Romans used them, too. They often waved their handkerchiefs as a way of greeting important people or applauding for actors in the theater. In later centuries handkerchiefs were very beautiful and were carried for display. Sometimes women gave a handkerchief to a man as a sign of affection.

Handkerchiefs were first used by early _____ of

wealth to mop their _____. Later, common citizens of

Rome used _____ to _____ at

important people. In more recent centuries handkerchiefs were

carried for _____ or given as signs of _____

Name

Critical Thinking, Level D © 1993 Steck-Vaughn

A. Classifying

Read each quote and decide if it would have been said in the early 1700s or today. Write **past** or **present** on the line in front of each quote.

_____ 1. "I will do this assignment on my computer."

_____ 2. "Sarah is working at the spinning wheel."

_____ 3. "How do you like my new digital watch?"

_____ 4. "The town crier is calling out the news."

_____ 5. "It's Sebastian's turn to get water from the well."

_____ 6. "Becky forgot to take her hornbook to school."

_____ 7. "We'll tape that TV show so we can watch it later."

_____ 8. "The cooper said the barrel will be ready today."

B. Fact and Opinion

Study the picture. Then read the sentences. Put **F** before each statement of fact and **O** before each opinion.

_____ 1. The wig is white.

_____ 2. The wig is very elegant.

_____ 3. We should wear wigs like that today.

_____ 4. The wig is full and curly.

_____ 5. Wigs are better than hats.

_____ 6. The wig is for a man.

Name _____

C. — Real and Fanciful

Read the story. Write an **R** above the pictures from the story that illustrate something that is real and an **F** above the pictures that illustrate something fanciful.

Caroline had been trying for some time, but she just couldn't get her kite to fly. The big white cloud floating above saw her and wanted to help. "I'll ask the wind to pick up her kite and make it fly," the cloud thought. But the wind was asleep and didn't like to be awakened. The cloud knew that if it upset the wind, the wind could blow it away.

"I know what I'll do," the cloud decided. "I'll ask the sun to wake up the wind. The wind always listens to the sun."

So the cloud spoke to the sun, and the sun woke up the wind. The wind blew just enough to make the kite fly but not enough to send away the cloud. Thanks to the cloud, the sun, and the wind, Caroline had great fun flying her kite.

D. — Outlining and Summarizing

Write a summary of the story above. Use another sheet of paper if

necessary. _____

_____

_____

_____

Name

Understanding

Understanding means telling about something in your own words. Look at the picture. What can you say about the two girls? Do you think they are friends? Why? What can you say about the baby? How do you know?

27

A. To **compare** things means to tell what is alike about them. To **contrast** things means to tell what is different about them. Look at the pictures of the two bedrooms and read the paragraph. Identify Anita's room and Heather's room.

    Anita and Heather both like to read. They both like to listen to the radio. Heather likes fancy things, while Anita likes things that have a simpler design. Anita lives in the city, but Heather lives in the country.

_____ room   _____ room

B. Use the information in the pictures and in the paragraph to answer these questions.

    1. What else is the same about Anita and Heather?

_____

_____

    2. How else are Anita and Heather different?

_____

_____

Name _____

Comparing and Contrasting

If you were to go back in time about 10,000 years, you might see some animals that look like the elephant of today. But you'd really be looking at mammoths and mastodons.

Mammoth

Mastodon

1. Compare and contrast the mammoth and the mastodon. How were the two animals alike?

_____

_____

_____

2. Complete the table by telling how the two animals were different.

	Mammoth	Mastodon
Size		
Head		
Tusks		

Name _____

A. On the lines below, explain how the items in each pair are alike.

1. snake and lizard _____

2. piano and harp _____

3. clock and watch _____

4. book and magazine _____

5. radio and television _____

6. roof and hat _____

7. sail and motor _____

8. candle and bulb _____

9. writing and talking _____

10. bird and kite _____

B. 1. Study the pairs in part A. In your opinion, which pair names things

that are most alike? _____

2. Which pair names things that are most unlike? _____

C. On the lines after the words below, write the names of two other items that are similar to each object named.

1. pencil _____   _____

2. pan _____   _____

3. flute _____   _____

4. shirt _____   _____

5. hat _____   _____

6. cup _____   _____

Name

The word **structure** refers to how something is built. A poem can be written by following a certain structure. Haiku is a type of Japanese poem that tells about something in nature and brings a certain feeling or mood to the reader. Haiku has its own special structure. For example, each line has a set number of syllables. Read the two examples of Haiku and then answer the questions about their structure.

Gently falling flakes
Blanketing the winter ground
Soft and wet and white.

Beating on the roof
Lightning flashing in the sky
Trees bent in the wind.

1. How many lines does each poem have? _____

2. How many syllables are in the first line? _____

3. How many syllables are in the second line? _____

4. How many syllables are in the third line? _____

5. Does Haiku have to rhyme? _____

Name _____

The structure of a story is the plan that is used to construct the story. Most stories follow a similar plan. It includes a setting, characters, and a plot. The **setting** tells the time and place of the story. The **characters** are the people or animals that the story is about. The **plot** is the sequence of events from the beginning, to the high point in the action, to a satisfactory ending.

From the list at the right, choose and write a plan for a story. Choose a time, place, and characters. Then write a sentence to show how you will begin, another to show the most exciting part of the action, and a third to tell how you will end the story. You may prefer to think of your own story parts.

long ago

last year

across the sea

on a ranch

deep in the forest

a girl on crutches

an adventurous boy

a wild pony

no one knew what happened

late one night

just as the hero

what a big splash

you can still see the spot

maybe some other time

Time _____   Place _____

Characters _____

Beginning _____

_____

High Point _____

_____

Ending _____

_____

Name

Critical Thinking, Level D © 1993 Steck-Vaughn

A **process** is the order in which something is done. Read the process described below. Then rewrite the sentences so that the steps are in the correct order.

Making a Bird Feeder

Punch four small holes in the plastic tray, one in each corner. Tie the four string ends together so your feeder will hang. Collect the materials you will need: a plastic tray from a supermarket package, 4 pieces of string about 20 inches long, peanut butter, cereal. Spread peanut butter on the bird-feeder tray. Knot each string at one end, and draw the other end through one of the holes in the tray. Sprinkle cereal, such as oatmeal, on the peanut butter. Hang your feeder and watch the birds enjoy it!

1. _____

_____

2. _____

_____

3. _____

_____

4. _____

_____

5. _____

_____

6. _____

_____

7. _____

_____

Name _____

33

A. Number the boxes to show the order in which the squares were shaded. Put **1** under the first box and continue with **2, 3, 4, 5, 6, 7,** and **8.**

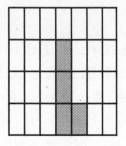   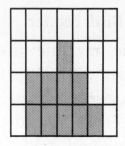   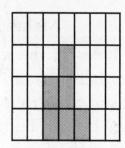   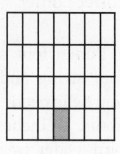

_____   _____   _____   _____

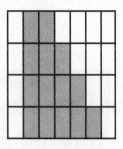   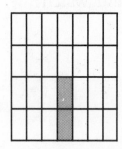   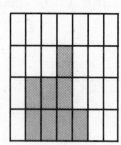   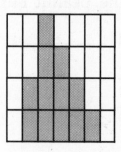

_____   _____   _____   _____

B. Tell the order in which you will make something. It may be an art project, some food, or whatever you choose. Write the title of your project on the first line. Then list six steps. Write the steps in order.

_____

1. _____

2. _____

3. _____

4. _____

5. _____

6. _____

Name _____

Critical Thinking, Level D © 1993 Steck-Vaughn

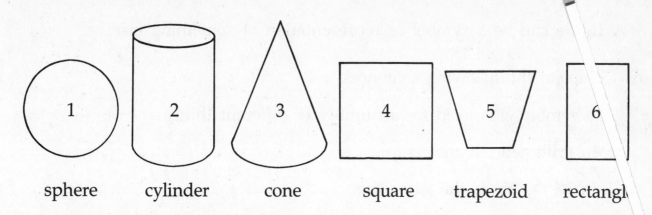

1 sphere 2 cylinder 3 cone 4 square 5 trapezoid 6 rectangle

When you study geometric shapes, you learn how to describe the world in mathematical language. In this drawing of part of an airport, you can find many geometrical shapes. Label each geometrical shape in the picture, using the numbers of the shapes shown above.

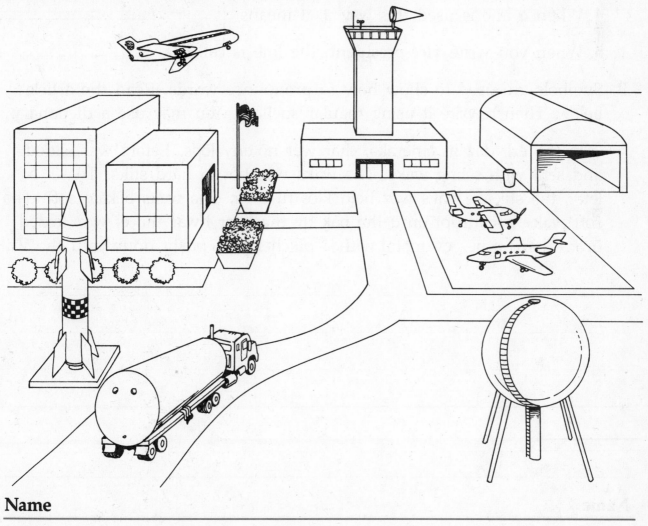

Name

A **figure** can be a symbol or representation of something else.

A. Complete the following sentences.

The symbol **X** is used for a number of different things.

1. In arithmetic, **X** means ––––––––––––––––––––––––––––––––– .

2. In **W**, **X**, **Y**, **Z**, the letter **X** is ––––––––––––––––––––––––– .

3. We could say, "**X** out the part that you do not want."

   This would mean –– .

Another symbol used for many things is a line: —.

4. When a line is used this way, **ā**, it means ––––––––––––––––– .

5. When you write **vice-president**, the line is called a ––––––––– .

B. Symbols are used to show how to pronounce words. Read the article below. Then rewrite it using regular spelling. You may use a dictionary.

   In ~~thə~~ érli daz in əmerəkə, ~~thâr~~ wér nō envəlōps. Letərz wér fōlded and sēld ~~with~~ sēling waks. ~~Thə~~ waks wəz bôt in härd stiks. Tü sēl ə letər, ~~thə~~ stik ov waks wəz held klōs tü ə fīr. ~~Thə~~ waks bēkām soft. ~~Thə~~ soft waks wəz dropt ontü ~~thə~~ bak ov ~~thə~~ letər hwâr ~~thə~~ ej wəz fōlded ōvər. ~~Then,~~ ə pēs ov metəl ~~with~~ ə pikcher wəz pusht doun intü ~~thə~~ waks.

––

––

––

––

––

Name ––––––––––––––––––––––––––––––––

Comparing Word Meanings

Homographs are words that are spelled alike but are not pronounced alike. Their meanings are also different.

In the pairs of sentences below, find the homographs and circle them. Put a check before each sentence in which the circled word has a long vowel sound. Then write a definition for each circled word that has a check before it.

_____ 1. Marge had a tear in the corner of her eye.

_____ Please do not tear the page in that book.

_____

_____ 2. The bird-watcher saw a beautiful dove.

_____ Janice dove into the deep water.

_____

_____ 3. Lester will read his report to the class.

_____ Ruth has read five library books this week.

_____

_____ 4. How long did your grandparents live in that town?

_____ Is that a dead wasp or a live one?

_____

_____ 5. You must wind the clock if you want it to work.

_____ There is a strong wind blowing toward us.

_____

Name _____

Each word in the box is the opposite, or **antonym**, of an underlined word in the sentences below. Write each word from the box on the line beside the sentence that contains its antonym.

tame	many	rough	straight	love	shout	push
lower	usually	quiet	leave	correct	foolish	false

1. _____ Mr. King polished the stone until it was shiny and smooth.

2. _____ Whisper when you tell me the secret.

3. _____ Few students are in the library now.

4. _____ Jennifer rarely rides the bus to school.

5. _____ Sam didn't want to give the wrong answer.

6. _____ Lions and tigers are wild animals.

7. _____ The scouts followed the crooked path through the woods.

8. _____ Pull the handle to open the drawer.

9. _____ Roger told me an unusual but true story.

10. _____ José asked Larry to raise the window shade.

11. _____ It's noisy in the school yard during recess.

12. _____ Sarah was wise to take her friend's advice.

13. _____ No one may enter the building until nine o'clock.

14. _____ Don't you hate to stay inside on a rainy day?

Name

_____

A. Choose the main idea for the story from the box. Write
   the sentence on the first line of the story.

> Early bicycles did not have pedals.
> Early bicycles were made almost
> entirely of wood.
> Early bicycles were hard to ride.

_____

The wheels were wooden. A wooden crossbar held the wheels together.
Another wooden crossbar steered these bicycles. Some wooden bicycles
were so rough to ride, they were called "boneshakers."

B. One test of a main-idea sentence is to see if the other sentences help to
   explain or develop it. Underline the sentence in each group below that
   best expresses the main idea of the group.

1. a. Wild turkeys live in small flocks in the woods.
   b. Turkeys build their nests on the forest ground.
   c. At night wild turkeys rest in trees.
   d. For food they eat wild nuts, berries, seeds, and insects.

2. a. Trace the design on a large bar of soap.
   b. Use a knife to cut the soap.
   c. Rub the soap lightly to take off any rough edges.
   d. Interesting figures can be carved from soap.

3. a. If danger is near, the mother springs away in big hops.
   b. Mother kangaroos protect their babies in many ways.
   c. Since young kangaroos are smaller than mice when they are born,
      they must stay in their mother's pouch for several months.
   d. Since mother kangaroos can run thirty miles per hour, they can
      outrun most of the animals that might harm their babies.

Name _____

The **main idea** of a paragraph may be found in the first or last sentence, or even in the middle of the paragraph. Underline the main-idea sentence in each paragraph below.

1.   Many accidents happen on sidewalks. People may fall over toys which have been left in the way. Muddy or icy spots may cause one to slip and fall. Holes in the cement also cause people to fall.

2.   The alligator dozes on the bank of the stream, appearing to be asleep. Suddenly it lashes out with its tail to kill some creature who is nearby. The alligator is sly when it comes to catching food.

3.   Although they are fascinating today, old-time trains were really quite uncomfortable to the passengers of long ago. The seats were rough and bumpy. The cars were open to wind, rain, and sun.

4.   Paper is made from wood. Medicine is made from bark. A tree is a very useful plant. Its leaves provide shade and beauty. Its roots soak up water which might have washed away soil.

Name

Critical Thinking, Level D © 1993 Steck-Vaughn

If a main idea is repeated in a slightly different way, its meaning will often become clear. In each paragraph below, underline the sentence that gives the main idea. Then put a check by the sentence you would choose to be the paragraph's closing sentence. The closing sentence should repeat the main idea stated in the sentence you underlined.

1.   The sea horse is a fish that isn't anything like a fish. It has a head like a horse and a tail that curls like a monkey's. It carries its young in a pouch like a kangaroo. It has bumps on its skin and can change color to hide from its enemies.

_____The sea horse is not your usual fish.

_____The sea horse got its name because it looks like a horse.

2.   The roadrunner is a flightless bird that has rattlesnakes for dinner. It kills the rattlesnake by kicking and pecking it. How does this bird manage to avoid the rattlesnake's deadly bite? The roadrunner moves very quickly. It can run as fast as 20 miles (32.2 km) per hour and jump as high as 10 feet (3m). So, when the rattlesnake tries to strike back with its fangs, the roadrunner can usually get out of the way in time.

_____ The most dangerous snake in the desert is the rattlesnake.

_____ This small bird is one of the rattlesnake's worst enemies.

Name _____

A. Study the picture. Then choose the main idea from the box and underline it.

People enjoy waiting in line at the bank.

People expect to wait in long lines at the bank.

People get upset if they have to wait in long lines at the bank.

B. Write five details from the picture that support the main idea you chose.

1. _____

2. _____

3. _____

4. _____

5. _____

Name _____

Critical Thinking, Level D © 1993 Steck-Vaughn

One thing often causes another thing to happen. This is called a **causal** (cause/effect) **relationship**.

A. Some causes and effects are listed below. Put the letter of the effect on the line before the most likely cause.

Causes	Effects
_____ 1. Hiking in the woods alone	a. supplies new scientific facts about the universe.
_____ 2. Being polite	b. keeps germs from spreading.
_____ 3. Cheering at a football game	c. sometimes saves you money.
_____ 4. An oil spill	d. helps you learn to work well with others.
_____ 5. Staying clean	e. makes other people happy.
_____ 6. Swimming	f. may kill sea life.
_____ 7. Sending astronauts into space	g. might cause you to get lost.
_____ 8. Playing on a team	h. may make your voice hoarse.
_____ 9. Digging many wells	i. may lower the level of water.
_____ 10. Growing your own vegetables	j. helps develop muscles.

B. Put **X** on the line before each sentence that shows a cause and effect relationship.

_____ 1. I tripped on the rug and hurt my knee.

_____ 2. Reading books often helps increase your knowledge.

_____ 3. We probably won't go tomorrow.

_____ 4. The snowstorm lasted most of the night.

Name

A. Place a check before the three sentences below that contain a cause-effect relationship. Circle the part in each sentence that contains the cause.

_____ 1. Rain fell all day Saturday, so we could not play outside.

_____ 2. Because the grass was becoming yellow, Mrs. Smith watered her yard yesterday.

_____ 3. Since it is so sunny and warm, we will go on a picnic.

_____ 4. Sixteen people left Sunday, but only fifteen people returned on Monday.

_____ 5. Tonight is cool and rainy, although last night was rather warm.

B. Complete each sentence by writing an effect that could result from the cause given.

1. Because of the violent storm, _____

_____ .

2. Jason was late for the party so _____

_____ .

3. After Deke had a big lunch, _____

_____ .

4. Since today is a holiday, _____

_____ .

5. Ling spilled popcorn on the floor _____

_____ .

Name _____

Critical Thinking, Level D © 1993 Steck-Vaughn

A. Comparing and Contrasting

Shapes may be alike even though they are turned around. Study each shape on the left. Then circle the shapes on the right that are the same as the one on the left.

1.

                        a.   b.   c.

2.

                        a.   b.   c.

3.

                        a.   b.   c.

B. Identifying Relationships

Three shapes in each group are related to one another. Find the shape that is different and put **X** on it.

1.

    a.   b.   c.   d.

2.

    a.   b.   c.   d.

3.

    a.   b.   c.   d.

Name

C. Identifying Structure

A **synonym** is a word that means just about the same thing as another word. To form the pairs of synonyms below, take a letter from the top word and use it to make a new word from the bottom word. Write the synonyms on the lines.

Example: tint   **tin**
meal   **metal**

1. boast _____    2. brush_____

   hip _____   tee _____

3. stalk _____   4. trip _____

   peak _____   ear _____

D. Comparing Word Meanings

Change the meaning of each word by adding one of the prefixes in the box.

super	semi	re

1. _____ call   2. _____ make   3. _____ private

4. _____ sonic   5. _____ port   6. _____ natural

7. _____ do   8. _____ circle   9. _____ read

Name _____

Applying

Applying means using what you know. Look at the picture. Where do you think the two girls are? Why is each girl wearing a number? Does the picture show what event they will take part in? Do the girls look like they are enjoying themselves? What do you think they might do next?

Arrange each list in order according to the directions above it. Write **1**, **2**, **3**, **4**, or **5** on the line before the word. **A** has been started for you.

A. from little to big

_____1_____ bee

_____ child

_____ cat

_____ bird

_____ whale

B. from fast to slow

_____ rabbit

_____ airplane

_____ turtle

_____ car

_____ spacecraft

C. from high to low

_____ house

_____ dog

_____ insect

_____ skyscraper

_____ refrigerator

D. from old to young

_____ baby

_____ toddler

_____ first grader

_____ grandparent

_____ teenager

E. from hot to cold

_____ rain

_____ fire

_____ ice water

_____ warm soup

_____ ice

F. from easy to difficult

_____ landing a plane

_____ giving a speech

_____ painting a picture

_____ riding a bike

_____ driving a bus

Name

Critical Thinking, Level D © 1993 Steck-Vaughn

Arrange the items in each group below according to size or amount, from smallest to largest. Write the items in order.

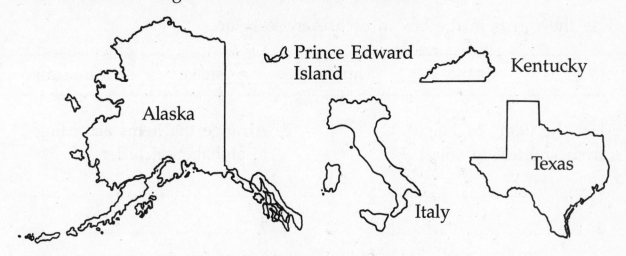

1. Alaska, Prince Edward Island, Italy, Kentucky, Texas

_____

2. 145, 115, 1045, 105, 150, 11054

_____

3. one-tenth, one-fourth, one-half, one-third, one-fifth

_____

4. marble, basketball, golf ball, baseball, beach ball

_____

5. baby, teenager, adult, child

_____

6. day, second, week, hour, weekend

_____

7. decade, year, century, month

_____

8. car, rollerskate, motorcycle, bicycle

_____

Name _____

There are many kinds of **order**. You can put the same things in different orders for different purposes.

Use the words in the box in each exercise below.

stool	horse	human	snake	mosquito

A. List the items by height, from shortest to tallest.

1. _____
2. _____
3. _____
4. _____
5. _____

B. Arrange the items according to alphabetical order.

1. _____
2. _____
3. _____
4. _____
5. _____

C. Arrange the items according to the number of legs each one has, from the smallest number to the largest.

1. _____
2. _____
3. _____
4. _____
5. _____

D. Arrange the items according to how much they eat, from the least to the most.

1. _____
2. _____
3. _____
4. _____
5. _____

Name _____

Critical Thinking, Level D © 1993 Steck-Vaughn

When you **estimate**, you make a guess that is based upon what you see or what you already know. In Parts A and B, you will use what you can see or what you already know to help you estimate.

A. The giraffe in the middle is ten feet (three meters) tall. Estimate the height of the giraffe on the left, the height of the giraffe on the right, and the height of the tree.

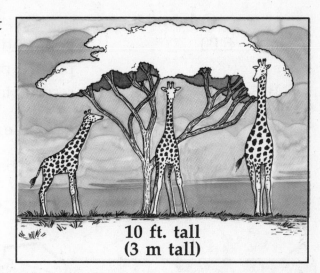

10 ft. tall
(3 m tall)

   Height of:

   1. Giraffe at left _____

   2. Giraffe at right _____

   3. Tree _____

B. Look at the map. It took Kevin 40 minutes to ride his bike from Glidden to Silver City. Estimate how long it will take him to ride from:

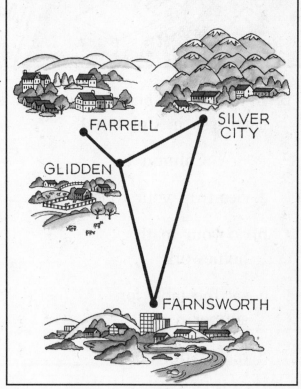

   1. Glidden to Farnsworth

   _____

   2. Glidden to Farrell

   _____

   3. Farnsworth to Silver City

   _____

Name _____

A. Estimate in your head the price of each item in **Column 2**. Then circle the item or items that you could buy with the amount of money listed in **Column 1**.

Column 1	**Column 2**
a. $ 5.00	pen, pad of paper, crayons, greeting card, picture frame
b. $ 10.00	record, tape, radio, watch, television
c. $ 25.00	gloves, earmuffs, coat, ski cap, boots
d. $ 50.00	pillow, bedspread, blanket, sheet, towel
e. $100.00	wagon, rocking horse, doll, electric train set, book

B. In **Column 2** below, write how long you think it would take you to do each task in **Column 1**.

Column 1	**Column 2**
a. clean up your room	_____
b. do your math homework	_____
c. set the table for supper	_____
d. make your bed	_____
e. write a letter to a friend	_____

Name _____

Critical Thinking, Level D © 1993 Steck-Vaughn

Some things are very likely to happen. These are called **probabilities**. Other things are unlikely to happen. They are not probabilities.

Read each statement. If it tells about something that is very likely to happen, write **probability** on the line before it.

_____ 1. Summer will be warmer than fall.

_____ 2. Miss Thomas, who is an actress, will have a lot to say about our play.

_____ 3. Mr. White will pay his bill next Friday because there is a penalty for paying after it date.

_____ 4. Melissa saw many black clouds in the sky on a sunny day.

_____ 5. Sarah has a broken leg and won't run in the race today.

_____ 6. You will celebrate your birthday sometime this year.

_____ 7. We will go swimming in the Arctic Ocean.

_____ 8. If your team plays ball against a team of high school students, your team will win.

_____ 9. If you exercise more than your friend, you will be stronger.

_____ 10. If you draw and paint well, you have talent in art.

Name _____

For each situation below, there are three different endings. Put **1** before the ending that is **most likely** to happen. Put **2** before the ending that could **possibly** happen. Put **3** before the ending that is **not very likely** to happen.

A. Rick is the smallest player on the basketball team. He practices often and is determined to be a good player. Rick will probably be

_____ the worst player on the team.

_____ about as good as the other players.

_____ one of the better players.

B. George has just moved to the city and does not know his way around the neighborhood. Late one afternoon, while walking down a street, he becomes so interested in the sights that he forgets to watch where he is going. He will probably

_____ feel lost and ask a police officer to take him home.

_____ wander around until he finds a familiar street.

_____ walk all evening until his family finally finds him.

C. It has always been difficult for Jane to write stories. She wants to improve, so she probably will

_____ ask a friend to help her.

_____ ask for help from her teachers at school.

_____ work with a professional writer from the newspaper.

Name _____

Critical Thinking, Level D © 1993 Steck-Vaughn

Using the information shown in the pictures, decide which explorer will probably get out of the cave first. On the lines below the pictures, explain your decision.

Picture 1

Picture 2

_____

_____

_____

_____

_____

_____

Name _____

Read the story. Then follow the directions below it.

The story of Rip Van Winkle takes place in the 1700's in the Catskill Mountains of New York. Rip was a farmer, but as his wife was always telling him, he was not a very good one.

One day Rip went out hunting in the woods. There he met a man dressed in old-fashioned clothing who was carrying a keg. Rip helped the man carry the keg up a mountain. At the top they met other men dressed like the first one. Rip and the men had a feast and then Rip fell asleep.

When Rip woke up, twenty years had passed. During this time Rip's wife had died and his children had grown up. Many other changes had taken place in Rip's village and in the country itself. The colonists had won the Revolutionary War and the United States was now an independent nation.

Imagine that you had an experience like Rip Van Winkle's and fell asleep for twenty years. What changes would probably take place during that time? Why do you think so?

_____

_____

_____

_____

_____

Name

Critical Thinking, Level D © 1993 Steck-Vaughn

To **infer** means to look at the evidence and come to a conclusion based on that evidence. That is, you look at the facts, and you **infer** the answer.

A. The sentences below give facts about objects. Infer what each object is, and write its name on the line.

———————— 1. It is long and narrow. It measures things. You may keep it in your desk.

———————— 2. You wear it outdoors. It does not cover a very large area of your body. You don't mind if it gets wet.

———————— 3. This is long and narrow, but it gets shorter each time you use it.

———————— 4. These objects glow and sparkle in the dark. We often see them in many colors on the Fourth of July.

———————— 5. You often carry this in a paper bag to school. You enjoy it at noon or when you go on a picnic.

———————— 6. This long stick has short bristles on one end. We are supposed to use it after meals and before we go to bed.

B. On the lines below, describe an object without naming it. Give facts that will enable a reader to infer what the object is.

————————————————————————————————

————————————————————————————————

————————————————————————————————

————————————————————————————————

————————————————————————————————

Name ————————————————————————————

Each group of pictures shows a silly race. The tracks made by the winner are also shown. Study the racers and the tracks carefully. Then write the winner on the finish line.

1.

The winner: _____

2.

The winner: _____

3.

The winner: _____

Name

Read each story and the sentences that tell about each person. Underline the sentence that tells who spoke.

1. The team is playing the last baseball game of the season. This is the last inning and the score is tied. The two players have struck out and now the bases are loaded. Someone says, "I'm sure I can help the team win with a base hit. I'll probably even hit a homer."

   a. Gus, who does not brag, is one of the team's better hitters.

   b. Lee has made many hits this year and is very sure of herself.

   c. Joe, the pitcher, has had one hit so far this year.

2. Last Thursday, Mr. Grant asked if someone would stay after school to help him clean the chalkboards. One student offered, "I will, Mr. Grant. You can count on me."

   a. Linda's brother was coming home today after spending two years in the navy.

   b. Rita's mother was going to the dentist and expected Rita to watch her younger brother after school.

   c. Lenny's parents both work until six o'clock and won't be home.

3. Terry didn't know that her friends were planning a surprise birthday party for her. She wondered why everyone stopped talking when she came by or why they giggled so much. She was also puzzled when someone said, "Terry, this will be a weekend you'll never forget."

   a. Ivan likes to brag.

   b. Jim has trouble keeping a secret.

   c. Cindy is jealous of Terry.

Name _____

A. Read the sentences. Write your inferences on the lines following them.

1. Wei has finished giving her oral book report, and she is smiling. The
   other students are clapping. _____

   _____

2. Sam keeps his boots in his locker. He has just come in from recess
   with wet feet. _____

   _____

3. Sandy's lunch is gone, and her books are missing. Sandy stopped to
   play on the way to school. _____

   _____

B. Sometimes you can draw different inferences from the same set of facts.
Write your own inferences for these statements.

1. Nell stops to examine a wound on her leg. She is wearing roller

   skates. A large dog is running down the street. _____

   _____

2. Eric is holding several packages from his favorite store. He is walking
   slowly with his neighbor, Mr. Grand, who has just recovered from an

   operation. _____

Critical Thinking, Level D © 1993 Steck-Vaughn

Name _____

In a **figure of speech** each word does not mean what it usually does. Instead, the words together have another meaning.

Read each sentence with a figure of speech. Then write what the sentence really means on the lines.

1. Earl was up to his neck in work.

_____

2. Ann wasn't dressed well today, but you shouldn't judge a book by its cover.

_____

3. My parents explained, "You must take care of your dog. You can't have your cake and eat it, too."

_____

4. It seemed as if Jeff had broken the wagon, but we may have been barking up the wrong tree.

_____

5. Robin jumped out of her skin when I dropped that book.

_____

6. We thought the comedian at the party was just a barrel of laughs.

_____

7. When the boys broke the window, they decided to face the music and tell the owner.

_____

8. Their lives hung by a thread as they battled the storm at sea.

_____

Name _____

A **prefix** is a group of letters added to the beginning of a word to change its meaning. The prefixes **un-**, **im-**, and **in-** are prefixes that change the meaning of a word to the opposite of its original meaning.

A. Add the prefix **un-**, **im-**, or **in-** to each of the words in the box. Write the new word and its meaning. Use a dictionary if you are not sure of a word.

Example: passable-impassable

| possible | accurate | fashionable | polite | clear |

1. _____

2. _____

3. _____

4. _____

5. _____

B. Write each word below **without** its prefix. Then give its new meaning.

1. unsafe _____

2. immature _____

3. immobile _____

4. inconsiderate _____

Critical Thinking, Level D © 1993 Steck-Vaughn

Name _____

A. Ordering Objects
Inferring

Read the paragraph and study the pictures. Then number the pictures **1** to **5** to show the correct order.

Shane lives at 122 Brick Lane. On his way to school he sees Mrs. Jaye's dog and then Mr. Gray's cat. Before long, Shane sees the school.

Name _____

B. Changes in Word Meanings
Estimating

Each of the pictures on this page represents a word with the word **can** in it. Write each word and its meaning below the picture that represents it. You may want to check a dictionary. Before you begin, estimate how long you think it will take you to complete this page. Write your estimate on the line. Then time yourself to see how close you were.

Estimated time: _____ Real time: _____

1.

_____

2.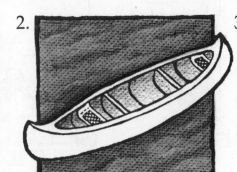

_____

3.

_____

4.

_____

_____

5.

_____

_____

6.

_____

_____

Name

_____

Analyzing

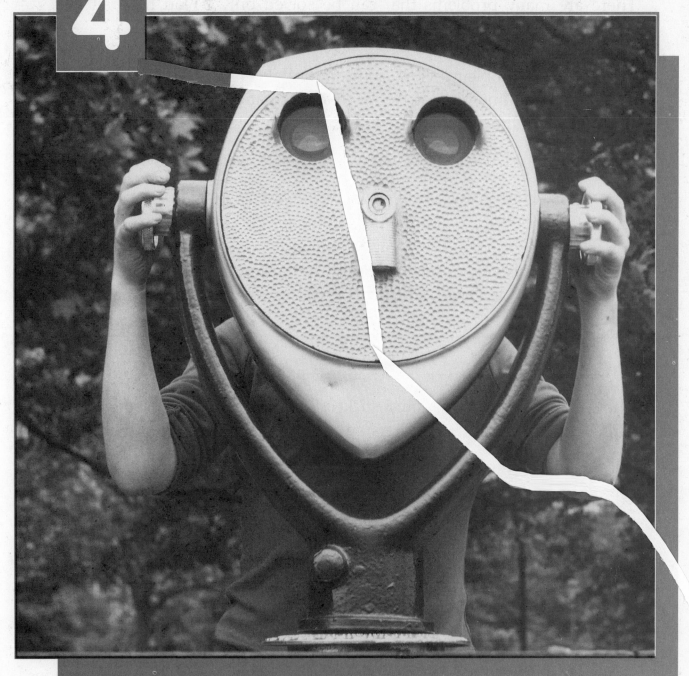

Analyzing means seeing how parts fit together. Tell what is happening in the picture. What is the person doing? How do you know? Why is the person looking through the machine? Would the person see as clear a scene without the machine? Can you tell what the person is trying to see?

There are many problems that can be solved only if you have all the necessary information, or **complete** information.

In each word problem below, some information is missing. Read the problem. On the line after it, write the information you would need before you could solve the problem.

1. Rosemary has 170 sheets of paper which she wants to divide among her classmates. How many sheets will each student get? _____

_____

2. Howard has sixteen postcards. David has fifteen, and Lee has more than either Howard or David. How many postcards do the boys have altogether? _____

_____

3. Theresa and Jenny have some stickers. Theresa has more than Jenny. The girls want to divide the stickers equally. How many stickers will each one get? _____

_____

4. Paul plans to buy a yo-yo for $1.50, some colored pens for $3.00, and some postage stamps. How much money will he need? _____

_____

5. Tammy travels 17 miles on the school bus each day. Gordon travels even more miles on his trip to and from school. How many more miles does Gordon travel than Tammy? _____

_____

Name _____

Critical Thinking, Level D © 1993 Steck-Vaughn

In a report, a writer should give exact and complete information.

A. Read the report below. Find and underline three sentences in the report that need more information.

Most people think that sand deserts are the only kind of desert. That is not true. Some deserts are covered in other ways besides sand. However, all deserts are alike in one way.

Desert plants and animals need little water. Some plants, such as the cactus, are well-suited for dry desert climates. The reason for this is interesting.

B. Use an encyclopedia or other reference book to find more exact information for the sentences you underlined in part A. Then rewrite the report, using the facts you have found to make the sentences more complete.

_____

_____

_____

_____

_____

_____

_____

_____

_____

Name _____

Sometimes you can fill in the facts to a story to make it complete by careful observation.

A. Study the picture carefully.
Then answer the questions.

1. What is happening in the picture?

_____

_____

_____

2. Explain why you think so.

_____

_____

_____

B. Suppose the house in the picture is yours, and you want to call the highway department in your town to tell them about the fallen tree. Write the complete information the people at the highway department will need to know so that the tree can be removed.

_____

C. Complete the paragraph about the picture in your own words.

The hurricane was very _____. The rain and

_____ caused a lot of damage. Most people stayed

home, but Dr. Brandon was out in his _____ making a

housecall. However a _____ kept him from getting

through. Mrs. Newman, who lived _____ nearby, came

out to see if she could help.

Name

Relevant information is information that is important to you.

Put a check by the two sentences that tell the most important things to do in order to successfully complete each activity.

1. Buy a bicycle

_____ Check the kind of tires the bicycle has.

_____ Compare the quality of different kinds of bicycles.

_____ Decide which one looks best.

_____ Visit some stores to compare prices.

2. Try out for beginners' band

_____ Tell the band teacher all about yourself.

_____ Let the band teacher know that your parents are musical.

_____ Follow directions carefully during the tryout.

_____ Be quiet unless you are asked to talk or play an instrument.

3. Make a project for the science fair

_____ Begin early so you will have enough time to work on it.

_____ Make a fancy project which uses only costly materials.

_____ Find a project you're interested in and can do by yourself.

_____ Help plan the science fair.

4. Race in the school track meet

_____ Practice every day for several weeks before the track meet.

_____ Enter every event that you can.

_____ Help your coach by being nearby when you might be needed.

_____ Do the best you can.

Name

Some scientists plan a trip to Antarctica and decide to take their families along. Suppose that your family is part of the group. Which five facts below will be most relevant to a family preparing for a stay in Antarctica? Put **R** before the five facts that seem most relevant to you.

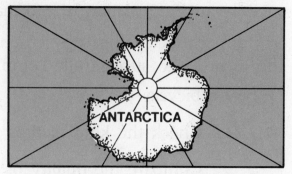

_____ 1. Heavy clothing is worn all year long at the South Pole.

_____ 2. Antarctica is a vast, frozen wasteland.

_____ 3. It is difficult to get supplies during some months of the year.

_____ 4. There are no highways in Antarctica.

_____ 5. The wind can be very destructive in polar areas.

_____ 6. You will spend a lot of time indoors in Antarctica.

_____ 7. Modern technology has helped to make cold areas more livable.

_____ 8. Seals, fish, whales, and penguins live along the Antarctic seacoast.

_____ 9. Antarctica is larger than Australia.

_____ 10. Frostbite can occur even when you are careful about protecting your skin.

Name _____

Critical Thinking, Level D © 1993 Steck-Vaughn

Some words are more general than others. For instance, the word **woman** is more general than the word **Judy**, because **woman** refers to a whole group of people and **Judy** refers to one person. When words are general, we say they are **abstract**. When words are specific, we say they are **concrete**.

A. Circle the more concrete word in each pair below. The first one is done for you.

1. gem, (diamond)   2. room, kitchen   3. clothes, suit

4. boy, Carl   5. food, steak   6. robin, bird

7. cat, animal   8. flower, rose   9. maple, tree

B. Number the words **1**, **2**, or **3** according to how concrete or abstract they are in relation to one another. The most concrete word in each group should be numbered **1**. The most abstract word should be numbered **3**.

1. _____ person   _____ boy   _____ Jesse

2. _____ rose   _____ plant   _____ flower

3. _____ cereal   _____ food   _____ oatmeal

4. _____ vehicle   _____ jeep   _____ car

5. _____ shoe   _____ footwear   _____ clothing

6. _____ water   _____ Atlantic   _____ ocean

Name

73

Abstract or Concrete

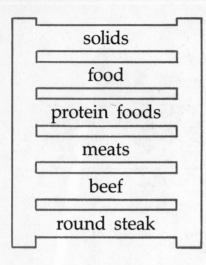

A very specific name of an item is on the bottom step of the ladder. As you climb the steps, you find names of broader groups or categories. On the top step is the broadest category into which all the other names belong.

Read the three lists of names below. Put each group in order by writing the names on the numbered ladders. Put the most specific name at the bottom, and the broadest name at the top.

1.

1. sweaters, outerwear, blue sweaters, clothes

2. birds, green parakeets, parrot family, parakeets, Tweetie (your parakeet)

3. house, shelter, buildings, split-level house, homes

2.

3.

Name

Logic of Actions

Read each problem or task. Then choose an item from the box that will help solve the problem or do the job. Write your choice on the line.

hammer	recipe	needle	saw	dime
pull toy	vase	bookmark	thermometer	rake
ice	rope	trash bin	toaster	ruler

_____ 1. You want to remove a splinter from your finger.

_____ 2. You need to know how much cinnamon to put in a fruit dessert.

_____ 3. You want to throw away some litter.

_____ 4. You need to tie down the flaps of a heavy box.

_____ 5. You want to mark a place in a story that you are reading.

_____ 6. You want a present for a one-year-old child.

_____ 7. You want to brown some bread for breakfast.

_____ 8. You want to arrange some flowers for the table.

_____ 9. You want to cut some logs for a fire.

_____ 10. You want to clean up the leaves in your yard.

Name _____

Read each statement. Put a check by the course of action that best completes each sentence.

1. Amy wanted to meet the new girl sitting on the steps across the street. When she saw her, Amy ————.

—————— watched her for a while

—————— went over and introduced herself

—————— went back into her house

2. Sabrina wanted to be good enough to play on the softball team, so she ————.

—————— practiced her hitting

—————— never went to any games

—————— met the team members

3. Mom's birthday was only a week away. Brian needed money to buy her a birthday present, so he ————.

—————— mowed his neighbor's lawn to earn money

—————— waited until he could save enough of his allowance

—————— told Mom he didn't have enough money

Name _____

Critical Thinking, Level D © 1993 Steck-Vaughn

Read the story below. Then answer the questions about it.

Cindy and Carla were nine-year-old twins who lived on a ranch. On the first Saturday of May, they brought their twin calves to the county fair. The girls groomed the little animals and then waited for the calf-judging contest to begin.

At last the contest was announced. The two girls, dressed alike in jeans and checked shirts, came out with their look-alike calves. The people in the stands thought they were seeing double!

Cindy and Carla won the top prize easily because the sight of the two sets of twins was so striking.

1. Who are the two main characters? _____

_____

2. Where and when does the story take place? _____

_____

3. What happens **first**, **next**, and **last** in the story? _____

_____

_____

4. How does the story end? _____

_____

Name _____

Read each story below.

I was born in a nest tucked away in a large barn. I have eleven brothers and sisters who were also born the same day I was. My brothers and sisters and I are white, and we have small pink eyes. (It was several days after we were born that we could open our eyes, however.) We also have long tails and fine whiskers. Now that we are a little older, we are beginning to explore our home. I think a barn is a dandy place for a little mouse to live!

Mr. Calvin decided to go for a ride in his new jeep. He invited Mac to go along with him. The two of them climbed into the jeep and set out for town. Mr. Calvin waved to friends and neighbors as they went by. People waved and called out, "Hi, Mac! Hi, Mr. Calvin!" Everyone admired the new jeep. At the Goode Foode Shoppe, Mr. Calvin got out and bought some yogurt for himself and for Mac. They sat on the curb and ate it. "You know, Mr. Calvin," said the man who owned the Goode Foode Shoppe, "I think it's nice that you treat your dog just like a person."

A. Write a title for each story.

1. _____

2. _____

B. Tell who the narrator, or voice, in each story is. Is it someone named in the story, or is it an outside narrator who sees the action but does not take part in it?

1. _____

2. _____

Name _____

Critical Thinking, Level D © 1993 Steck-Vaughn

Study the pictures below. Number them **1** to **4** so that they are in a logical order. Then, under each picture, write a sentence or two to tell what is happening.

_____

_____

_____

_____

_____

_____

_____

_____

Name _____

If a sentence is **logical**, it makes sense. It fits correctly with the information that comes before it.

Read each group of sentences below. If the last sentence is logical, put a check before the number.

Example: Parrots can learn to talk. Greenie is a parrot. Greenie can learn to talk. (The last sentence is logical because it fits correctly with the information before it. It makes sense.)

_____ 1. All of my friends like to swim. Bobby is my friend. Bobby likes to swim.

_____ 2. Many animals have brown-and-white coloring. Candy has a beautiful dog. Candy's dog is brown and white.

_____ 3. Anita does not like to be around wasps. Arnold has wasps by his house. Anita doesn't like to go to Arnold's house.

_____ 4. Most plants are green. The holly fern is a plant. The holly fern is probably green.

_____ 5. Tom does not like school very much. Elsie does like school. Tom and Elsie don't like each other.

_____ 6. Many people have brown hair and brown eyes. George is a person. George has brown hair and brown eyes.

_____ 7. Some students in this school are female. The other students are male. There are more females than males in this school.

_____ 8. Kathy is always on time. Kathy is coming to my house. Kathy will be punctual unless something unexpected happens.

Name _____

Critical Thinking, Level D © 1993 Steck-Vaughn

An **analogy** is a special kind of comparison.

In each analogy below, decide how the first two words are related. Then relate the second two words in the same way by choosing a word from the word box.

alphabet	climb	king
mountain	light	foot
bottom	dig	soup
island	find	pool

1. **clean** is to **dirty** as **top** is to _____

2. **run** is to **track** as **swim** is to _____

3. **creek** is to **river** as **hill** is to _____

4. **finger** is to **hand** as **toe** is to _____

5. **feel** is to **touch** as **discover** is to _____

6. **drum** is to **band** as **letter** is to _____

7. **bang** is to **noise** as **flash** is to _____

8. **girl** is to **boy** as **queen** is to _____

9. **broom** is to **sweep** as **shovel** is to _____

10. **stove** is to **cook** as **ladder** is to _____

11. **frame** is to **picture** as **water** is to _____

12. **glass** is to **milk** as **bowl** is to _____

Name

In some analogies the second pair of words is not related in the way that the first pair is. Such analogies are called **false analogies**. Look at the example below.

Example: night is to **moonlight** as **day** is to **school**

The first two words, **night** and **moonlight**, show the relationship that the last two words must have in order for the analogy to be true. But the words **day** and **school** do not have the same relationship that the words **night** and **moonlight** have, so the analogy is false. In order for the analogy to be true, the last term must be **sunlight**.

A. Read each analogy below. Underline each false analogy.
   1. **person** is to **house** as **bird** is to **nest**
   2. **book** is to **read** as **pencil** is to **measure**
   3. **hand** is to **glove** as **foot** is to **sock**
   4. **ice cream** is to **cold** as **hot chocolate** is to **breakfast**
   5. **mother** is to **father** as **aunt** is to **nephew**

B. The last word of each analogy below is missing. Write the word that will complete the analogy correctly.

   1. **sun** is to **day** as **moon** is to _____

   2. **water** is to **liquid** as **ice** is to _____

   3. **spaghetti** is to **eat** as **coat** is to _____

   4. **light** is to **dark** as **below** is to _____

   5. **chair** is to **sit** as **bed** is to _____

   6. **field** is to **football** as **court** is to _____

   7. **book** is to **read** as **television** is to _____

   8. **sidewalk** is to **pedestrians** as **street** is to _____

Name _____

A. Some "either-or" statements are true because, at times, only two choices are possible. But some "either-or" statements are false because there could be more than two choices to consider. Write **true** or **false** before each "either-or" statement below. The first one is done for you.

_____false_____ 1. Water is either hot or cold.

_____ 2. A house pet is either a dog or a fish.

_____ 3. A president is either young or old.

_____ 4. The lights are either off or on.

_____ 5. Your hair is either blonde or brown.

_____ 6. Either you like to work or you don't like to work.

_____ 7. The store is either open or closed.

_____ 8. Winter weather is either snowy or rainy.

B. For each false statement above, write the number of the statement and list some other choices which should have been included. The first one is done for you.

1. warm, cool, boiling, lukewarm

_____

_____

_____

_____

_____

Name _____

A **loaded word** is one that plays on your emotions in order to persuade you to think, do, or buy something.

A. Read the advertisements below and circle the loaded words.

> **Example:** Bonny Wipes are a real (bargain) for (clever) shoppers. Try these (new) and (improved) tissues.

1. I was ashamed of my embarrassing dandruff until I used Flakeoff.

2. My new Dirtyrinse does a fantastic job on clothes.

3. Gobble removes the toughest stains faster and easier.

4. A smart shopper like you can't afford to miss this special sale.

5. Seethrough is softer and more absorbent than other towels.

6. This is your last chance to save money on a Hotstuff Water Heater.

7. The year's best value is this Safari Flashlight.

8. Bones Plus gives your dog special nutrition and extra calcium.

B. Use the lines below to write an ad for pet skunks. Use loaded words to try to persuade your readers that skunks make terrific pets!

_____

_____

_____

_____

_____

Critical Thinking, Level D © 1993 Steck-Vaughn

Name

A. —Judging Completeness

All the things pictured below were returned to the store because they were incomplete. Under each item write what is missing.

1.   2.   3.

4.   5.   6.

B. —Abstract or Concrete

Notice the dark words in each sentence below. Put **1** above the word that is most concrete. Continue numbering the words up to **4** so that the most abstract word is numbered **4**.

1. Mrs. Norton wanted some **accessories** for her new outfit, so she

    stopped at the **jewelry** counter to look at **earrings** and selected a pair

    of **drop earrings**.

2. Helen took her **coat** back to the **clothing** store because a **slicker** was

    not the kind of **outdoor gear** she wanted.

Name

C. Story Logic

Read the story below and circle the words that are not logical.

Becky and her family moved to a farm in 1870. Their apartment house was near a large shopping mall. Becky's father cleared the land around the house and planted some crops. When Becky wasn't helping out on the farm, she went swimming in the ocean with friends or rode around town on her skateboard. On Saturdays, she and her family sometimes went to the movies in their station wagon.

D. Logic of Actions

Check the items in each list below that would be logical for pioneers to do.

1. Pioneers made their own

_____ clothes

_____ candles

_____ home movies

_____ brooms

2. Pioneers lived in

_____ trailers

_____ apartments

_____ log cabins

_____ sod houses

3. Pioneer scouts learned to

_____ walk quietly

_____ use snowmobiles

_____ track animals

_____ use walkie-talkies

4. For fun, pioneers

_____ watched TV

_____ square danced

_____ told stories

_____ sang songs

Name

Critical Thinking, Level D © 1993 Steck-Vaughn

Synthesizing

**Synthesizing means putting information
together to come up with new ideas.**
Look at the picture. What are the girls
doing? Can they understand each other?
How do you know? Is one learning from
the other? Why or why not? What are
some other ways people communicate?

Communicating Ideas

A **rebus** is a kind of puzzle in which pictures are used in place of words or parts of words. The rebus below uses pictures for syllables.

A. Draw a picture for each missing syllable in the rebuses below. The first is done for you.

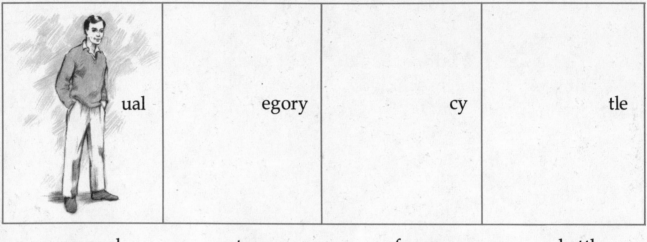

| ual | egory | cy | tle |

1. ___manual___   2. ___category___   3. ___fancy___   4. ___battle___

B. Underline five words in the paragraph below that you can picture. Then rewrite the paragraph using rebuses for those words.

Herb filled his cup with hot water from the teapot. Then he sat down to read the paper and enjoy his tea. When Herb took his first sip, he said, "Ugh!" He had forgotten to put a teabag into his cup.

_____

_____

_____

_____

_____

Name

If you have ever placed a classified ad in the newspaper, you know that it costs more money to show a longer ad. Many people shorten, or abbreviate, longer words in these ads. For example, **CA** is used to mean central air-conditioning. You probably won't find most of these abbreviations in a dictionary. Read the ads below and try to guess the meaning of each abbreviation. Then rewrite the ads, using the correct spelling of each word.

1.
> Hse for sale; 2 bdrms, ba, kit,
> dng rm; lrg porch & bk yd;
> wood w/ brk trim.

_____

_____

_____

_____

2.
> Apt. for rent w/ dbl gar & sw
> pool; CA; 3 BR, 2 BA; Kit-Din
> area; Bsmt; wlk-in clst.

_____

_____

_____

_____

Name _____

Each pair of thermometers below has a numeral beside it. The first numeral stands for a temperature on the Celsius scale. Use a red pencil to show how far the mercury must rise to reach that temperature. The second thermometer in each pair has a numeral which stands for the same temperature on the Fahrenheit scale. Use a blue pencil to show the mercury on that thermometer.

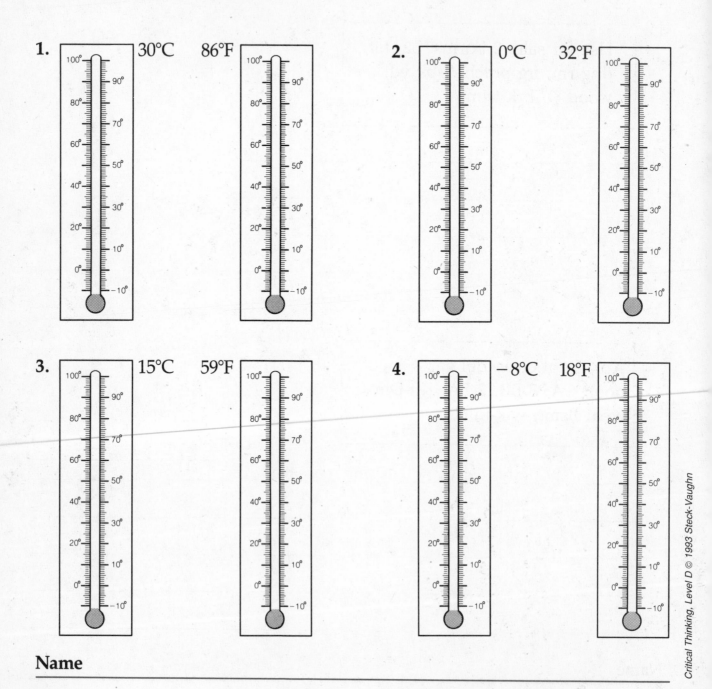

Name _____

When you plan a project, you collect the tools or equipment you will need, decide on the goals you want to achieve, and make a plan of action to follow.

Read the activities below and put checks before the answers you choose. Each question has more than one correct answer.

1. Your teacher has asked your class to make posters which show the effects (results) of air pollution. Which of the following things will students need to make posters?

_____ colored markers   _____ rulers   _____ paints

_____ encyclopedia   _____ tape recorder   _____ yarn

_____ poster paper   _____ brushes   _____ pencils

2. Suppose you are one of the three judges in a contest to decide who is the fastest runner in your class. Which of the following things will be most helpful in deciding the winner?

_____ a tape measure to judge the distance by

_____ a stopwatch to time the race

_____ a book about running

3. You are going to a department store to buy gifts for the holidays. Which things would be the most useful?

_____ a shopping list of names and possible gifts

_____ money

_____ comfortable shoes for walking

_____ an address book

_____ stamps

Name

Read the story below and complete the activity following it.

World Biker

In the 1880s the bicycle had a large wheel in front and a tiny one in the back. The thing was difficult to ride in the city and almost impossible in the country.

In spite of the poor bicycle, Thomas Stevens decided he would pedal his way around the world. At the time he made up his mind to make the trip, he didn't even know how to ride a bicycle. He practiced a few days and was off.

He began in San Francisco in April 1884. In August, after 5000 kilometers of rough road and trouble, he arrived in Boston. There, he persuaded a bicycle manufacturer to pay for the rest of his trip.

Then Stevens sailed across the ocean and rode through Europe. By the time he got to Asia, he was loaded down with gifts.

By January 1887, Stevens was back in San Francisco and still had his bicycle! He was famous by that time. After that he made money giving lectures.

Suppose you were going on a bicycle trip around the world. Which things listed below would you consider necessary to take with you? Write **1** for those you think more necessary and **2** for those that are less necessary. Leave the line blank if you don't think the item is important at all.

_____ toothbrush	_____ maps	_____ medicines
_____ money	_____ helmet	_____ soap and towel
_____ backpack	_____ blanket	_____ tent
_____ extra clothes	_____ pen and paper	_____ goggles
_____ bicycle tools	_____ food	_____ water canteen

Name

Critical Thinking, Level D © 1993 Steck-Vaughn

A **hypothesis** is an explanation of why something may have happened. A hypothesis is built upon facts that are given to you. Sometimes the same set of facts can lead to different hypotheses.

Below each story are three hypotheses that explain why the situation in the story may have happened. Read the story. Then put a check before the most likely hypothesis. Then, on the writing lines, give still another hypothesis of your own.

1. One summer night, Jeff left his bicycle out in the front yard. The next morning, he found that his bicycle was all wet.

   _____ a. It rained during the night.

   _____ b. The evening dew made the grass and the bicycle wet.

   _____ c. The bicycle was parked near a lawn sprinkler that had been left on all night.

   _____

   _____

2. Tina and Alex discovered that the library corner was in a mess. Some books were leaning on the shelves. Others had fallen to the floor.

   _____ a. The children had been careless about putting books on the shelves. As a result, some books had fallen off.

   _____ b. The books had not been neatly stacked in the beginning.

   _____ c. The pegs which hold the bookshelf had slipped and caused the books to fall.

   _____

   _____

Name _____

95

Read each group of sentences. Answer the questions by writing your own hypothesis.

1. Our basement is flooded. I think someone left the faucet on. What else could have caused the flooding?

_____

_____

2. When Pam and her friend came home from school yesterday, they noticed cars parked up and down both sides of the neighborhood street. Pam thought it might be a party, but the people looked unhappy. What else might have been happening?

_____

_____

3. Ants keep coming into the kitchen. My parents think some jam or jelly is spilled in the back of a shelf. What else could account for the ants?

_____

_____

4. Our rose bushes used to have big blooms. Now they just have little ones. Roberto thinks we didn't fertilize them. What other reason could there be?

_____

_____

5. Hui says the dog is scratching itself all the time. Maybe the dog needs a bath. What else could cause the scratching?

_____

_____

Name _____

A. Read the story. Then check the sentence that gives the most likely reason for what happened.

Randy was good at making fruit punches. One day she made a punch with grape juice. She added fresh fruit to the juice and served it to her friends. Everyone thought it was good. The next time Randy made a grape juice punch, she added sugar to the mixture. Her friends said the punch was too sweet. The third time that Randy made grape juice punch, she used fresh fruit and seltzer. Randy's friends liked this punch best of all.

Why was the second punch unsuccessful?

_____ Her friends liked the first punch better.

_____ The grape juice already had sugar in it.

_____ Randy's friends don't like sweet drinks.

_____ It didn't have seltzer in it.

B. How do you think that Randy could make another sweet punch which her friends would like? Write your ideas on the lines.

_____

_____

_____

_____

Name _____

Building Hypotheses

Read the paragraph. Then use clues to build a hypothesis.

Betsy has been gone from her room for a few minutes. She returns to find that the apple she left on her desk isn't there. Betsy sees some clues that might explain what happened to her apple.

1. Look at the picture. What clues do you see?

_____

_____

2. What hypothesis might you build from these clues?

_____

_____

_____

Name _____

Critical Thinking, Level D © 1993 Steck-Vaughn

Read each story. Then write a conclusion about how the trip will turn out. Tell why you think so.

1. Our class is going ice-skating on Sudbury Pond. We hope the ice is thick enough! Some of the students don't have skates, but they think they can borrow some. Janet says you're supposed to call the park department and get permission, so one of us will probably do that. We're wondering if we're allowed to have a bonfire to keep warm.

Conclusion _____

Why do you think so? _____

_____

_____

_____

2. Our class has planned a trip to the zoo to see how different animals are adapted to their homelands. We have arranged for a bus to take us there and back. We will each bring a bag lunch and will buy something to drink at a refreshment stand. We have each read about a different animal and will make a point of seeing that animal. Some of us are bringing cameras, and each of us will take notes.

Conclusion _____

Why do you think so? _____

_____

_____

_____

Name _____

Read each story. Then check the sentence under it that gives the best conclusion for each.

1.   Leroy folded up the lawn chairs and put them in the shed. He brought the potted plants indoors. He also put the garbage cans in the garage. Leroy checked to make sure nothing else was loose in the yard. Then he went inside and listened once more to the reports on the radio.

_____ Leroy is going away on vacation.

_____ Leroy is expecting a big storm.

_____ Leroy has heard that a criminal is loose.

2.   Miss Trinidad hunted all over the house. The longer she looked, the more upset she became and the more she squinted. Finally, in exasperation, she put her hand to her head. How Miss Trinidad smiled when she realized what a silly mistake she had made!

_____ Miss Trinidad found she was wearing her eyeglasses.

_____ Miss Trinidad's headache went away.

_____ Miss Trinidad realized she was wearing her missing ring.

3.   Duncan got in the elevator and pushed the button. When the door opened, he trudged wearily to his apartment door. It took Duncan several minutes before he realized that his key just wouldn't fit into the lock. When he looked up, he saw why.

_____ Duncan had the wrong key.

_____ The lock on the door was broken.

_____ Duncan had gotten off at the wrong floor.

Name _____

Critical Thinking, Level D © 1993 Steck-Vaughn

Read each group of sentences that tells something about Theodore Roosevelt. Then answer the question about your conclusion.

1. Theodore Roosevelt, the 26th president of the United States, often used the word *bully*. When he was given permission to form the Rough Riders, a special army regiment, he said, "Bully!"
    Upon hearing that he had just been elected president by the greatest popular vote up to that time, he said, "That's bully!"

    What conclusion can you draw about Theodore Roosevelt's use of the word *bully*?

    _____

    _____

    _____

2. "You must control Alice," a man advised Roosevelt.
    "I can do one of two things," Theodore Roosevelt replied. "I can be President of the United States, or I can control my daughter Alice. I cannot possibly do both."

    What conclusion can you draw about Alice Roosevelt?

    _____

    _____

    _____

Name
_____

Look at the cards below.

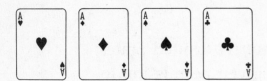

Notice that only one card has a heart on it. If a friend were to turn all the cards face down and mix them up, you would have **one chance out of four** (one in four) of picking up the card with the heart on it. You can make this conclusion because only one of the four cards has a heart on it.

1. If you wanted to fix it so that your friend would have **one chance in three** of picking the card with a heart on it, how many cards of different suits would you place upside-down? _____

2. If the cards below were turned face down and mixed up, what chance would you have of picking the card with two hearts on it?

_____

Was your conclusion **one chance in ten**? That is correct.

3. Now decide what chance you would have of picking out the card with one heart if the cards below were turned upside-down and mixed up.

_____

Name

Critical Thinking, Level D © 1993 Steck-Vaughn

Proposing Alternatives

Before you solve a problem, you should think of several alternate ways to handle it and choose the best one. Read about the problems below. Check the alternative to handle each problem which you think is better than the others. Then, on the lines, write another good alternative.

1. You are home alone in a first floor apartment. Suddenly, water starts dripping on you from the ceiling. The people who live upstairs are away on vacation. You should:

   _____ call your parents at work and ask them what to do.

   _____ find the building caretaker if you can.

   _____ get a ladder and try to get into the upstairs apartment by opening an unlocked window.

   _____

   _____

2. You rode the bus to the shopping center on a rainy day. You spent all of your money on toys and food. Now it is time to go home and you have no money for bus fare. You should:

   _____ walk the eight miles in the rain.

   _____ go back to the store where you bought several toys and try to return one of them.

   _____ tell the police officer on the block what has happened.

   _____

   _____

Name _____

Read each story. Then write two ways that the person in the story might solve the problem.

A.   Bill Johnson was worried as he walked home from school. Last week the teacher allowed Bill's friend Jack to change seats. Now, Jack sat directly behind Bill.

Jack's move caused a problem. Every few minutes, Jack leaned forward and whispered to Bill. Bill had trouble getting his work done.

Yesterday, the teacher talked about the science fair. Because Jack was whispering, Bill was not sure what the students were supposed to do.

1. _____

_____

2. _____

_____

B.   Georgia wanted a certain blue sweater for her birthday. Her older sister said she would buy it for Georgia. So Georgia described the sweater and told her sister where to get it. When her birthday came, Georgia eagerly opened her sister's present. Her sister watched in satisfaction. Imagine Georgia's surprise when the sweater in the box was not the one she wanted. Georgia knew her sister had gone to a lot of trouble and she didn't want to hurt her feelings; still, she was disappointed. She was not sure what to do.

1. _____

_____

2. _____

_____

Name

Critical Thinking, Level D © 1993 Steck-Vaughn

A. Your parents have given you permission to cut up some old magazines. How would you use magazines for the projects listed below? Write your ideas on the lines.

1. For the bulletin board at school _____

_____

2. For a written report _____

_____

3. For a greeting card you'll make _____

_____

4. In a booklet you want to assemble _____

_____

B. Your grandmother has said you may have some of her old scraps of cloth. Tell how you would use them in the following projects:

1. In an art project _____

_____

2. In a sewing project _____

_____

3. In a cleaning project _____

_____

4. In a game _____

_____

Name _____

Proposing Alternatives

A. Study each item pictured below. Then think of alternate ways to use it. Write your ideas on the lines.

1.

_____

_____

2.

_____

_____

3.

_____

_____

4.

_____

_____

5.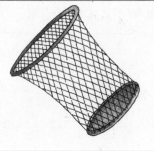

_____

6.

_____

B. Think of a common item that you use all the time. Then draw a picture to show an alternate way of using that item.

_____

_____

Name _____

Critical Thinking, Level D © 1993 Steck-Vaughn

A. —Planning Projects

To conduct a scientific project, a scientist follows certain steps. Study the comic strip below. Then write under each panel the correct step from the box.

_____

_____

1. Begin with the problem.   4. Do the experiment
2. Develop a hypothesis about how to solve it.   5. Study the results.
3. Collect the information you need.   6. Develop a conclusion.

Name _____

B. Building Hypotheses

Mr. Ramonte came into this room and took three things—a flower, some sheets of music, and his eyeglasses. Write a hypothesis to explain why. Use clues from the picture to help you.

_____

_____

_____

C. Proposing Alternatives

The electricity has gone off in your house because of a storm. Write an alternate action for each of the following tasks.

1. vacuuming the rug _____

2. mixing batter in the blender _____

3. watching television _____

4. ironing your clothes _____

5. turning on the air conditioner _____

Name _____

Critical Thinking, Level D © 1993 Steck-Vaughn

Evaluating

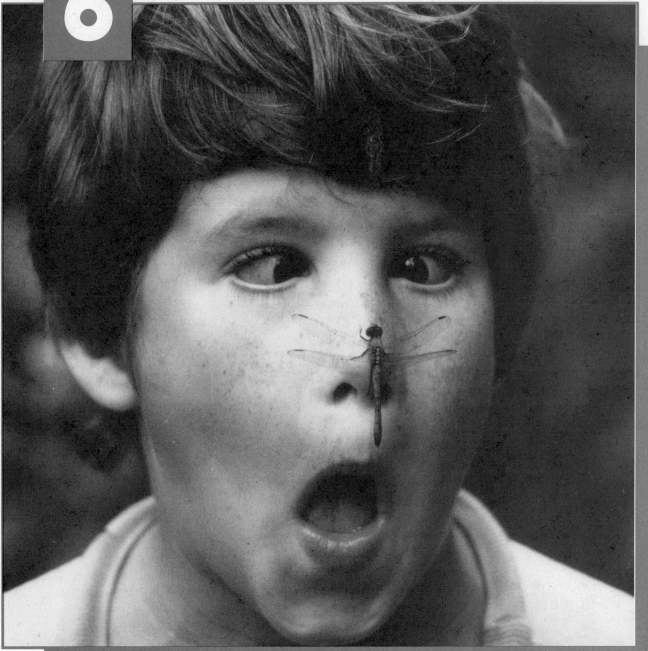

Evaluating means making a judgment or decision about something. What is happening in the picture? What does the boy's expression tell you? Did he expect the dragonfly to land on his nose? How do you know? Would you like to have the same thing happen to you? Why or why not?

109

A good **generalization** is a statement that is true for all the details that lead up to it.

A. Read each statement and the words which follow. If the statement is true for **all** of the words, write **T** on the line. If the statement is not true about **one** of the words, write **F** on the line.

_____ 1. These items can be used to tie something.
    rope   string   ribbon   cord   wire

_____ 2. These animals are covered with feathers.
    chicken   robin   ostrich   peacock   dolphin

_____ 3. These are different kinds of workers.
    teacher   writer   electrician   carpenter   florist

_____ 4. These articles can be found in a kitchen.
    refrigerator   cabinets   dishes   car   stove

B. Three meanings are given for each word below. If all three meanings are correct for the word, write **T** on the line. If only two of the meanings are correct, write **F** on the line. You may use a dictionary.

_____ 1. **chest:** a part of the body; a box with a lid; a piece of furniture.

_____ 2. **seal:** to close tightly; a sea animal; a gumdrop

_____ 3. **shower:** a kind of bath; a party for someone; light rain

_____ 4. **tied:** fastened; made the same score as someone else; arranged in a knot or bow

Name _____

Critical Thinking, Level D © 1993 Steck-Vaughn

Read the story below and complete the activity that follows it.

Dinosaur footprints are a rare sight to many people. However, near Price, Utah, they are very common. Dinosaurs walked in the soft sand and clay of eastern Utah millions of years ago. Their footprints are found in the coal mines in the area.

There are large prints which were left by an adult tyrannosaurus, and small prints left by a young one. Right down the middle of both footprints are marks left by the big tail of the adult and the tiny tail of the smaller one.

The prints of the meat-eating tyrannosaurus and the plant-eating brontosaurus are so common in Price that many residents walk by them every day without noticing them.

Copy the words that make each sentence an accurate generalization.

1. The area where Price, Utah, is now located was once

   a. very dangerous.
   b. full of dinosaurs.

   _____

2. The tyrannosaurus and the brontosaurus

   a. did not like the same food.
   b. ate green plants.

   _____

3. The dinosaurs left footprints because

   a. the clay and sand were soft.
   b. the ground was wet.

   _____

4. Dinosaur footprints around Price, Utah, are

   a. like those in most towns.
   b. unique to that area.

   _____

Name _____

Each of these generalizations states something that is not always true. Write a sentence of your own to prove that the generalization is not always true.

Example: All animals on a farm are raised for food.
A farm dog is a pet.

1. All basketball players are over six feet tall.

_____

2. All people who own cars know how to drive.

_____

3. Parties are always fun.

_____

4. Flowers bloom only in spring and summer.

_____

5. All television shows are violent.

_____

Critical Thinking, Level D © 1993 Steck-Vaughn

Name

A **criterion** is a rule, or guideline, that you use for judging something. (The plural of **criterion** is **criteria**.)

A. Your family has told you that you can have a new pet. Here are the criteria your family has given:

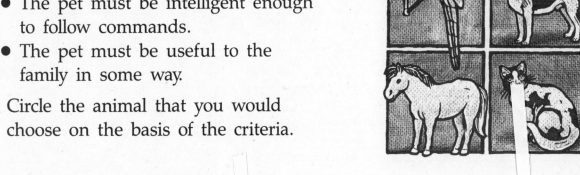

- The pet must be small enough to keep indoors.
- The pet must be intelligent enough to follow commands.
- The pet must be useful to the family in some way.

1. Circle the animal that you would choose on the basis of the criteria.

2. Tell why you circled that animal.

_____

_____

B. You are going to learn how to play a musical instrument. These are your criteria:

- You want to be able to play it in a band.
- You want it to be in the brass family.
- You want something that isn't too heavy to hold.

1. Circle the instrument that you would choose on the basis of the criteria.

2. Tell why you circled that instrument.

_____

_____

Name _____

Developing Criteria

Suppose that your class is going to have a science fair. You need to develop some criteria for this event. Your class has agreed that there will be entrance requirements about who can take part. There will also be requirements for the way the exhibits are set up. On the lines below, make a list of criteria that you think would be useful for a good class science fair.

1. _____

_____

2. _____

_____

3. _____

_____

4. _____

_____

5. _____

_____

Name _____

When you read or listen, ask yourself if what is written or said makes sense. Sometimes people say one thing and then another that is just the opposite. It is difficult to determine what they really mean.

Read these paragraphs. Find the sentences in each that **contradict**, or say the opposite thing. Underline these contradictory sentences.

1. The first known crossword puzzle appeared in the year 1913. It ran in a newspaper called the **New York World**. An editor of the paper, Arthur Wynne, made up the puzzle. It had 32 words and was in the shape of a diamond. No one is sure who wrote the puzzle.

2. The **New York World** was also a leader when it came to the nation's first comic strip. In 1893 the newspaper published a full color comic called "Hogan's Alley." It introduced a set of humorous characters to the paper's readers. The colorless page was not very funny. The public soon cried for more.

3. William Randolph Hearst published a comic strip called "The Yellow Kid" in his paper, the **Morning-Journal**. This was the first comic to use speech balloons for dialogue. It is not known who the publisher of the newspaper was.

Name

115

Sometimes when people speak or write, they are not exact in the words that they use. This makes it hard to understand just what they mean. You cannot make good judgments about things if you do not know what is really meant.

Read the paragraph. Find five examples of a word or phrase that is not exact. Underline these examples. Then rewrite the paragraph using more exact words for those that you underlined.

The wind blew a lot. The sky was darkish. Some clouds were sort of moving in our direction. We were kind of worried. Things did not seem so good.

_____

_____

_____

_____

_____

Name

When you judge something, you come to a conclusion about it. It is important that your conclusions make sense. When you make a conclusion, base it on the facts that are given.

Read the two paragraphs. Underline the concluding sentence in each paragraph. Then circle the conclusion that does not follow the facts given.

Carmen slowed down and tried to calm herself as she approached Fred's yard. She smiled weakly at Fred's dog, Romp, when he barked at her. Then, she walked as quickly as she could up to the door and rang the bell. When Romp followed her and tried to lick her hand, Carmen jumped and pulled it away. Carmen did not like Romp.

Carmen slowed down and tried to calm herself as she approached Fred's yard. She smiled weakly at Fred's dog, Romp, when he barked at her. Then, she walked as quickly as she could up to the door and rang the bell. When Romp followed her and tried to lick her hand, Carmen jumped and pulled it away. Carmen was afraid of Romp.

Reread the sentence that you circled. In your own words, write why this conclusion does not make sense with the facts given.

_____

_____

Name_____

(Judging Accuracy)

When you write a report, you get information from different sources. It is important to make good choices about the sources you use.

Read the paragraph below. Then fill in each blank with one of the sources given in the box. Choose the best source for each sentence.

globe	encyclopedia	poem	chart
newspaper	dictionary	television	interpreter

From looking at a _____, you can tell that China has many neighbors. According

to a current _____ , only one other country in the world has more land than China. That country is Canada.

On a _____ showing world population, you can see that China has more people than any other nation. China also has the world's oldest living civilization. A recent

program on _____ showed that the Chinese were the first people to develop the compass, paper, silk, and fine china. China also has an old and great body of literature and painting. Many of the paintings are a kind of fine handwriting called **calligraphy**. The

_____ says that it is pronounced **kə lĭg′ rə fē.** This ancient art is still practiced today.

Name _____

Critical Thinking, Level D © 1993 Steck-Vaughn

There are often many ways to do something. Some ways are better than others. It is a good idea to stop and think about all the possibilities before you decide.

Each sentence tells about what someone wants to do. The three sentences that follow give ways that this could be done. Underline the sentence that you think tells the best way.

1. Nora doesn't have enough money to buy flowers for the table of a fall party she is giving.

   a. She could use a green houseplant.
   b. She could use autumn leaves.
   c. She could make a centerpiece.

2. Jim wants to remember to call his grandmother on a certain date to wish her a happy birthday.

   a. He could tie a string around his finger.
   b. He could mark the date on a calendar.
   c. He could write a note to himself and put it in a place he always looks.

3. Nigel wants to buy a used bicycle.

   a. He could ask his friends if they want to sell theirs.
   b. He could check the local classified ads for bicycles.
   c. He could ask at the bike shop to see if they have any.

4. Brett wants to find an original way to thank his neighbor for a weekend at the seashore.

   a. He could write a thank-you note.
   b. He could go over and thank the neighbor in person.
   c. He could give the neighbor a scrapbook of photos he took during the weekend.

Name

Read the sentences. Each tells about what someone wants to do. Decide what you think is the best way to solve the problem. Write your idea on the lines.

1. Yuri accidently got locked out of his house. No one else is home. Yuri is upset because he has a lot of homework to complete as well as a test to study for. What should Yuri do?

_____

_____

2. Maggie went to the store to buy a few groceries for her mother. At the checkout counter, she realized that she had far too much to carry home. What should Maggie do?

_____

_____

3. Ray looks out the window and sees fresh-fallen snow on the ground one morning. He wants to share the beauty of this with his pen pal in Hawaii who has never seen snow. What should Ray do?

_____

_____

Name _____

Read each story and answer the question.

1.　Tomorrow Nathan would fly his kite in the kite-flying contest. While eating dinner, he remembered his kite was outside. He decided that he'd get it after he finished dinner. Then he noticed there were dark clouds in the sky, and it was very windy. Nathan decided not to wait. He went outside and got the kite. The next day Nathan won the kite-flying contest.

How might the story have ended if Nathan had made a different

decision? _____

_____

_____

_____

2.　Samantha had planned to practice her jumps for the ice show, especially the last, most difficult one. Her friends were going to a new movie, and she decided to go with them instead. At the ice show the next day, she performed her jumps well, except for the last one. She made a bad landing and fell to the ice.

How might the story have ended if Samantha had made a different decision?

_____

_____

_____

_____

Name _____

Read the paragraphs. Put a check by the decision you would make. Then explain why you made that decision.

You live in Australia, where there are many kangaroos. You've seen kangaroos leap as high as six feet (1.8 m) and hop at speeds up to 40 miles (64.4 km) per hour.

You decide to care for a baby kangaroo, called a joey, whose mother was killed. You get a permit to care for a wild animal. Then you find out how to take care of the joey and what it will need.

As the joey grows under your care, it becomes a member of your family and is very tame. However, by the time it is one year old, it can live very well on its own. Now you must make a decision. You want to do what is best for the kangaroo. What should you do?

1. _____ Get a permit so the kangaroo can stay with you longer.

_____ Return the kangaroo to the wild.

_____ Take the kangaroo to a nature preserve for wild animals.

2. Why do you think you made the best decision?

_____

_____

_____

_____

Name _____

Values are standards of behavior that people feel are important.

A. Some values—words and their definitions—are listed in the box. Below the list are five sentences that give examples of people living by these values. On the line following each sentence, write which value is being shown.

courtesy	kindness, respect for others
courage	meeting danger and bad times bravely
affection	love, friendship
rectitude	honesty, fair play

1. When the art supplies were bought, all the students honored their promise to contribute to the cost. _____

2. Ms. Jameson always has time to listen to our ideas. _____

3. Judy put her arm around her best friend, Cindy, on their way home from school. _____

4. Mr. Lenez faced his operation without complaining. _____

5. Kuang found a dollar bill on the playground and turned in the money to the principal. _____

B. Write a paragraph listing the qualities you value most in a friend.

_____

_____

_____

Name _____

Read the story. Then write three things you think Trudy might do. Check the one you think she **should** do.

Trudy selected a fancy pen and some greeting cards at the card shop. She got in line to pay for her things. When it was her turn, Trudy put her purchases on the counter. The woman behind Trudy put her things on the counter, too. Trudy noticed that the woman was buying a cute notepad. She wished she had enough money to get one.

While Trudy was getting out her money, the clerk put her things in a bag. Trudy paid, thanked the clerk, and left. When she got home, Trudy found that the clerk had put the notepad in her bag with her other things by mistake.

"Maybe the clerk wanted you to have it," said Trudy's brother. "You did want it, and I'm sure the shop has lots of these pads. Anyway, it wasn't **your** mistake. Why should you have to go to the trouble of taking it back? They might not believe you!"

Trudy wanted to keep the pad, and she didn't have time to take it back today. Still, Trudy wasn't sure what to do.

1. _____

_____

2. _____

_____

3. _____

_____

Name _____

Critical Thinking, Level D © 1993 Steck-Vaughn

Part of the **mood** of a story is based on the feelings of the characters.

Read each paragraph. Make each sentence in parentheses correct by circling the word that shows what the character is feeling.

"Ay, ay!" groaned Little Turtle. He was thinking about his father, Big Wolf. Big Wolf was not pleased with Little Turtle. (Little Turtle was: **hopeful, worried, carefree**.)

Little Turtle hung his head. He would have to tell Big Wolf the reason why he was late. He had been grinding corn for his grandmother. (Little Turtle was: **tired, contented, sad**.)

He loved his grandmother. She was gentle and wise. She was the best teller of tales in the whole village. But Big Wolf never seemed to understand all this. (Little Turtle was: **happy, foolish, disappointed**.)

"So that is why you are late!" Big Wolf exclaimed. "You can find time to work for others, but you do not do your own work." (Big Wolf was: **friendly, angry, calm**.)

Just then a woman ran up to Big Wolf and cried, "My small child is lost in the desert. No one has found her. I fear for my child's safety." (The woman was: **concerned, doubtful, grateful**.)

Little Turtle was alarmed. The child could not live long in the hot desert without water. He ran off to find her. (Little Turtle was: **mad, confused, courageous**.)

Little Turtle returned some time later with the lost child. Then Big Wolf said to him, "I see you are wiser than I am in some ways. You know that helping others is sometimes more important than helping yourself." (Big Wolf was: **unfair, kind, proud**.)

Name _____

Mood of a Story

A story's mood can be created by the setting, or where the story takes place.

Read the paragraph. Then answer the questions.

The waves pounded the shore, bringing the ocean a little closer to Buzz with each new onslaught. He watched as the white froth eddied around his sand castle, then reluctantly dropped back, only to return seconds later with the next wave. It was too cold to swim today and too rough. Yet Buzz thought these gray, windy days at the beach were the best of all. It was then, he felt, that the ocean really showed its strength. As another wave broke away part of the castle, Buzz shivered. It was comforting to know that he was here on the shore, not far from the cottage, and not out at sea where the waves ruled unchallenged.

1. How would you describe the place where Buzz is? _____

_____

2. What kind of day is it? _____

_____

3. How does Buzz feel? _____

_____

Name

Critical Thinking, Level D © 1993 Steck-Vaughn

A. — Developing Criteria

Study each picture and the information that goes with it. Then answer the question.

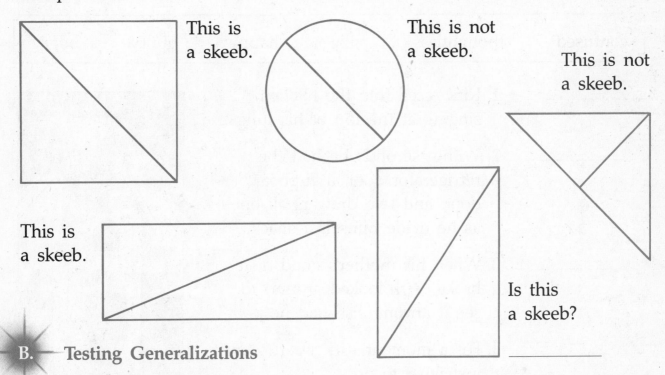

This is
a skeeb.

This is not
a skeeb.

This is not
a skeeb.

This is
a skeeb.

Is this
a skeeb?

_____

B. — Testing Generalizations

If the generalization about skeebs is true, write **true**. If the generalization is not true, write **false**.

1. Skeebs must have four sides. _____

2. A skeeb can be a circle. _____

3. A skeeb must be a square. _____

4. All skeebs have a diagonal line dividing them into two equal parts.

_____

5. Skeebs must have only straight lines. _____

Name
_____

C. — Mood of a Story

Read each sentence of the story. Choose a word from the box that best fits the emotion or action of the character. Write the word on the line.

confused	thoughtless	silly	happy	guilty	angry

_____ 1. Kirk raced into the kitchen, singing at the top of his lungs.

_____ 2. Within seconds he had the refrigerator door, a cupboard door, and two drawers all open as he made himself a snack.

_____ 3. When his mother's good dish broke, Kirk looked around to see if anyone else had noticed.

_____ 4. For a moment Kirk wasn't sure just what to do.

D. — Identifying Values

Write a paragraph in which you tell Kirk what to do.

_____

_____

_____

_____

_____

Name _____

Critical Thinking, Level D © 1993 Steck-Vaughn